Twayne's English Authors Series

EDITOR OF THIS VOLUME

Arthur Kinney

University of Massachusetts

Sir John Suckling

TEAS 218

Sir John Suckling
by Sir Anthony Van Dyck

SIR JOHN SUCKLING

By CHARLES L. SQUIER

University of Colorado

TWAYNE PUBLISHERS

A DIVISION OF G. K. HALL & CO., BOSTON

Published in 1978 by Twayne Publishers,
A Division of G. K. Hall & Co.
All Rights Reserved

Printed on permanent/durable acid-free paper and bound
in the United States of America

First Printing

Library of Congress Cataloging in Publication Data

Squier, Charles L.
Sir John Suckling.

(Twayne's English authors series ; TEAS 218)
Bibliography: p. 165 - 67
Includes index.
1.   Suckling, John, Sir, 1609 - 1642
—Criticism and interpretation.
PR3718.Z5S6   821'.4   78-6429
ISBN 0-8057-6721-5

For
Jan, Alison, and Chuck

Contents

About the Author

Preface

Chronology

1. "Natural, Easy Suckling": The Life   13

2. The Prose: A Bright and Elegant Surface   33

3. The Plays: *The Sad One* and *Aglaura*   57

4. The Plays: *The Goblins* and *Brennoralt*   76

5. Poems: Finding a Voice (1626 - 1632)   96

6. Poems: The Poet as Lover (1632 - 1637)   115

7. Poems: The Social Voice (1637 - 1641)   135

8. "Right Worthy of His Honours": Reputation,
   Influences, and Achievement   149

Notes and References   157

Selected Bibliography   165

Index   168

About the Author

Charles L. Squier received his undergraduate training at Harvard, where, after military service, he also earned an A.M.T. He received his Ph.D. in English literature from the University of Michigan. He is currently an associate professor of English at the University of Colorado, Boulder, where he has been teaching since 1963. At Colorado he has taught courses in Shakespeare, seventeenth-century literature, modern poetry, and in creative writing.

He coedited *The Sonnet*, Washington Square Press, and has published articles on American poetry and Renaissance drama. He has published poetry and fiction in a number of journals and has been a participant in the Poets-in-the-Schools Program in Colorado.

During the academic year of 1974 - 75 he taught at the University of Liverpool, England, as a visiting lecturer.

Preface

Sir John Suckling has written a handful of poems which will be read with pleasure as long as English is read. Such an achievement alone would justify a critical examination of his work; but Suckling, perhaps better and more interestingly than any of the Cavalier poets, captures the style of an era, not just in his poetry, but in his plays and in his prose as well. He was not a weighty, "serious" author; but his urbane wit, humor, and style make him something more than just a writer of light verse. The argument of his work is the argument of style, and Suckling's style offered a highly personal and civilized response to the great civil, religious, and social stresses of his day.

Suckling's brief and tragic life underlines the tragedy of his times, and this study begins with a discussion of his life and an overview of his literary activity. Next, a chapter is devoted to his most neglected work, his prose. Then come two chapters on his plays. The succeeding three chapters, which adopt the canon and dating established by Thomas Clayton in his edition of Suckling, consider his most important and interesting poems.[1] The final chapter presents a brief evaluation of Suckling's merits and his place in English literature. Relatively little has been written about Suckling, but the bibliography presented here is selective. Works of peripheral interest or limited value to the general reader are omitted.

No one can read and study the work of Sir John Suckling without expressing gratitude for the scholarship of the editors of the excellent Oxford edition, Thomas Clayton and L. A. Beaurline, and of his biographer, Herbert Berry. My colleague at the University of Colorado at Boulder, Professor H. D. Kelling, has given me helpful criticism for which I am grateful. My wife has provided invaluable help.

I wish to acknowledge the assistance of the Council on Research and Creative Work of the University of Colorado in providing a Faculty Fellowship and of the Department of English in providing assistance for the preparation of the manuscript.

The quotations from John Aubrey's *Brief Lives*, ed. Oliver Lawson Dick, are printed with the permission of the University of Michigan Press. The quotations from *The Works of Sir John Suckling, The Non-Dramatic Works*, ed. Thomas Clayton, and *The Plays*, ed. L. A. Beaurline, 1971, Oxford University Press, are printed by permission of The Clarendon Press, Oxford. The photograph of the Van Dyck portrait of Suckling is reproduced with the permission of the Frick Collection, copyright, The Frick Collection, New York.

CHARLES L. SQUIER

University of Colorado—Boulder

Chronology

1609   John Suckling is born in Goodfathers, Whitton, Middlesex, and is baptized in the church of St. Mary the Virgin on February 10.

1613   Suckling's mother dies on October 28.

1616   His father is knighted by King James on January 22.

1623   He matriculates as a fellow commoner at Trinity College, Cambridge, in the Easter term.

1627   His father dies. Suckling probably joins Lord Mountjoy's cavalry troop for the expedition to the Ile of Rhé commanded by the Duke of Buckingham.

1629   He travels in the Low Countries, studies astrology at Leyden University, and is possibly in military service with Lord Wimbledon.

1630   He is knighted by King Charles at Theobald's on September 19.

1631   From October until spring 1632 he is in the service of Sir Henry Vane, King Charles's ambassador to Gustavus Adolphus, in Germany.

1634   Suckling's unsuccessful courtship of a likely heiress, Anne Willoughby, ends in a quarrel.

1637   *Aglaura, An Account of Religion by Reason*, "The Wits" ("A Sessions of the Poets") are written. *Aglaura* is produced at court during the Christmas season.

1638   *Aglaura* is lavishly produced at Blackfriars and at the Cockpit Theater and published in folio. Suckling probably writes "A Ballade. Upon a Wedding" this year. He sells his last estate, Roos Hall, and is appointed a Gentleman of the Privy Chamber Extraordinary.

1639   He raises his "troope of 100 very handsome young proper men" for the First Bishops' War. The Treaty of Berwick is signed.

1640   He is Member of Parliament for Bramber, Sussex, from April 30 until Parliament is dissolved on May 5. Commissioned a captain for the Second Bishops' War, Suckling and his troop retreat with the rest of the army after the defeat at Newburn Ford near Newcastle. He writes *The Goblins* and *Brennoralt* about this time as well as the political tract, *To Mr. Henry German, in the Beginning of Parliament, 1640.*

1641   Suckling is involved in the "Army Plot" and flees to France on May 6. He dies in Paris sometime before the end of the year, probably by taking poison.

1646   *Fragmenta Aurea. A Collection of All the Incomparable Peeces, Written by Sir John Suckling. And Published by a Friend to Perpetuate His Memory.*

1659   *The Last Remains of Sir John Suckling. Being a Full Collection of All His Poems and Letters Which Have Been So Long Expected, and Never Till Now Published.*

CHAPTER 1

"Natural, Easy Suckling": The Life

I The Little Thing Well Done

IN 1675, thirty-four years after Sir John Suckling's death, Edward Phillips described him in *Theatrum Poetarum* as ". . . a witty and elegant Courtier under his late Majesty, his poems . . . have a pretty touch of a gentile Spirit, and still keep their reputation with any writ so long ago; his plays also still bring audience to the Theater."[1] Of course Suckling's plays have long ceased to attract audiences and are but seldom read; otherwise Phillips's commentary remains pertinent and in part valid. Suckling's poems do indeed "still keep their reputation with any writ so long ago." "Witty and elegant" aptly describe the man and his poetry. The aristocratic, courtly, and fashionable quality of his work is properly suggested by "a pretty touch of a gentile Spirit."

He is the embodiment of the Cavalier spirit of unstrained, negligent wit, charm, and grace. And it is as such that William Congreve's heroine Millamant thinks of him in her musings on "Natural, easy Suckling" in *The Way of the World*. Millamant's "natural and easy," however, along with Phillips's "more of the grape than Lamp," are not helpful if they are seen to imply an elegant trifler effortlessly tossing off brilliant *vers de société* between drinking bouts and love affairs. Suckling's achievement was to make the difficult seem easy, to mask his art with the appearance of casual and unlabored naturalness, to do, in short, exactly what the courtier poet was expected to do. Suckling is, as James Flosdorf has observed, "a conscious artist, and not, as has often been thought, a poet who merely dashed his poems off carelessly."[2]

On the other hand, Suckling is often seen, and correctly so, as the artist of the little thing and of the social moment.

I pray thee spare me, gentle Boy;
Presse me no more for that slight toy,
That foolish trifle of an heart;
I swear it will not do its part,
Though thou dost thine, employ'st thy power and art.[3]

These are the lines Millamant recalled in *The Way of the World*
and they surely have "a pretty touch of a gentile Spirit" in all their
easy grace. But Millamant quite properly did not quote the last
stanza of the poem with its libertine cynicism:

And oh! when once that course is past,
How short a time the Feast doth last!
Men rise away, and scarce say grace,
Or civilly once thank the face
That did invite, but seek another place.
(52, 16 - 20)

But the cynicism is as much a part of the poet as the urbane
charm. Beneath the shining surface there is an underlying
toughness and skepticism, even perhaps a great darkness. Ernest
Rhys's comment, "Suckling is a poet who in this gallery of tame
pigeons sits apart, with blood upon his gay feathers,"[4] points to a
quality in Suckling which makes him more than just a skilled writer
of society verse, something more than just another one, in Alexander Pope's phrase, of the "mob of gentlemen who wrote with
ease."

This is not to say, however, that Suckling's poetry is complex and
difficult to interpret. The reverse is so, and L. A. Beaurline has
isolated a significant critical paradox for the student of Suckling's
poetry:

Sir John Suckling's song "Why So Pale and Wan Fond Lover" is one of the
most famous lyrics in English. . . . But to the critic it is a challenge—obviously a fine poem; yet what can a critic say about it? Beyond an appraisal
such as "How clever!" what language do we have to describe the poem's
excellence? We are embarrassed by its simplicity; if we cannot show its
complexity or illuminate its obscurities we feel the poem is inconsequential.
Among academic critics especially, such a tendency exists because of the
need to have "something to talk about" to a class of students.[5]

Beyond this simplicity and openness of Suckling's poetry there is

an additional problem for the contemporary reader. Confronted
with

> Why so pale and wan fond Lover?
> Prithee why so pale?
> Will, when looking well can't move her,
> Looking ill prevaile?
> Prithee why so pale?
>
> (64, 1 - 5)

today's student may well be willing to admit that the poem is lively
and entertaining, but still feel a bit of impatient indignation. First
the question may seem peculiar. Next, even when the tradition of
the Petrarchan lover is explained, the poem may still appear strange
and distant. Its origins are in tradition and the play on tradition, not
in feelings or emotions. It is impersonal. If the critical question of
what to say about the poem is solved, some readers still may ask,
why say anything about it all? It is too slight for concern, these
readers will argue, asking what we are doing studying this elegant
trifle while cities rot and smolder, the air and the streams reek with
pollution, and the great missiles sit, snug and silent in their concrete
revetments.

Eventually the answer is that given by William Butler Yeats in
"Lapis Lazuli":

> One asks for mournful melodies;
> Accomplished fingers begin to play.
> Their eyes mid many wrinkles, their eyes,
> Their ancient, glittering eyes, are gay.[6]

The art and the artifact transcend the transient moment. The great
value of Suckling's poetry is in the way of the saying and in the
recognition of the artistry and its role in keeping the darkness at
bay. But beyond these general assertions about significance, we
must look specifically at Suckling himself and his work to see what
we can find of use and delight in this poet of a few brilliant poems,
this poet of a brief and particular moment in the history of English
literature.

II   *"This Gentile and Princely Poet"*

Sir John Suckling is hardly an autobiographical poet, but his work
needs to be read and understood in the context of his life and times.

As is the case with the work of any artist, Suckling's is influenced by
the traditions of his era, by public and private events, as well as by
his own genius. James Flosdorf has correctly remarked that "he is at
once conventional and rebellious against convention,"[7] and certainly one of the advantages of strong poetic conventions lies in the
ways one may work against them. Nonetheless, some of Suckling's
rebelliousness may be attributable to his life.

   A glance at the chronology of that life shows at once its brevity
and˙ its paucity of substantial worldly achievement. Humphrey
Moseley, the publisher of *Fragmenta Aurea*, those "golden
remains" of 1646, and *The Last Remains of Sir John Suckling*
(1659), wrote in the prefatory material to the latter: "Among the
highest and most refin'd Wits of the Nation, this Gentile and
Princely poet took his generous rise from the Court; where, having
flourish'd with splendour and reputation, he liv'd only long enough
to see the Sunset of that Majesty from whose auspicious beams he
derived his lustre, and with whose declining state his own loyal Fortunes were obscured."[8] The lines have all the hyperbolical inflation
of a good publisher's blurb, but even so they manage to suggest the
melancholy circumstances of Suckling's life. In part those circumstances were such as were shared by all those who attached
themselves to the Stuart cause.

>   Tourneyes, Masques, Theaters, better become
>   Our *Halcyon* dayes; what though the German Drum
>   Bellow for freedome and revenge, the noyse
>   Concernes not us, nor should divert our joyes;
>   Nor ought the thunder of their Carabins
>   Drowne the sweet Ayres of our tun'd Violins;
>   Beleeve me friend, if their prevailing powers
>   Gaine them a calme securitie like ours,
>   They'le hang their Armes up on the Olive bough,
>   And dance, and revell then, as we doe now.[9]

Lines such as these by Suckling's friend Thomas Carew need hardly
be taken seriously as political commentary or as a sober assessment
of England in 1632, but they do serve to locate the attitudes which
define the Cavalier pose and make it at once absurd and poignant.
However one may disapprove of the sillier postures of the Caroline
aristocracy, the game was shortly to end and many good men would
lie dead on the fields of England. If the king marched forward to
the block with absolute obstinacy and stunning obtuseness, the

bleakness of his end is no less tragic; nor is it less heroic.

Within the context of a whole society doomed to failure, Suckling's private life appears as pathetic and tragic as any. That "generous rise" Moseley speaks of is hard to find. Like most of his fellow courtiers he purchased his knighthood and his court post. He led his glorious troop of cavalry to the comic opera of the First Bishops' War, but it cost him dear in money and reputation. His involvement in political and military intrigue, the so-called Army Plot which was to end in his flight to France and his suicide there, hastened the very end Suckling and his comrades hoped to prevent, the execution of Thomas Wentworth, Earl of Strafford. His attempts to marry for love or for money were unsuccessful and, in at least one instance, embarrassingly scandalous. Although his most recent biographer, Herbert Berry, notes that Suckling "was one of the few English poets who was by profession a gambler . . . ,"[10] he also records the sad succession of gambling losses that eventually wiped out all his substantial patrimony. (Berry even believes that Suckling did not invent cribbage, a social contribution traditionally ascribed to him. Thomas Clayton, however, contests this view.) His suicide in the obscurity of Parisian exile gives further emphasis to the sense of failure in his life. The epitome of courtly gaiety, wit, and ease disappears from the scene, dies most probably by his own hand, in poverty in a foreign country.

III *The Early Years*

Suckling's life began auspiciously with the convenience of a wealthy and well-placed father. He was born in February 1609 at Twickenham, outside of London, where his father, also John Suckling, had an estate at Whitton. His father was a vigorous and active courtier who eventually became a member of the Privy Council and held the positions of Master of Requests and Comptroller of the King's Household. Although he did not succeed in achieving the Chancellorship of the Exchequer or the post of Secretary of State, for which he strove mightily, John Suckling the elder was a very successful and substantial courtier. Suckling's mother, Martha, was the sister of Lionel Cranfield, who was to become Lord Treasurer of England and Earl of Middlesex. Martha Suckling died at the age of thirty-five in 1613. Although Suckling's father married again in 1616, the role of a mother must have been played, in part, at least, by his eldest and favorite sister, also named Martha.

Suckling's father owned Roos Hall in Suffolk and later the manor house of Barsham, Suffolk, as well as other country properties, but Suckling appears to have been brought up principally in London and its vicinity, living mainly in the family house in Dorset Court or at the family estate at Whitton. His poetry certainly is the work of a city dweller and indicates no love for the country. Nothing is known of his childhood. Gerard Langbaine's statement that Suckling "spoke Latin at Five Years old and writ it an Nine"[11] would indicate precocity, but may or may not be true. Theophilus Cibber's report that he was born "with a remarkable circumstance of his mother's going eleven months with him"[12] seems questionable, but not very helpful one way or another. There are no records of his preuniversity training; it is quite likely that he received it from private tutors. The first record of his education is that of his matriculation as a fellow commoner at Cambridge from Trinity College in the Easter term of 1623.

It is difficult to believe that the young Suckling devoted himself to his studies with great assiduity. He left Cambridge without a degree, but this was a common enough practice. One may assume that he mixed pleasure and study with liberal proportions of the former, but it would be foolish to assume he was totally idle. Nonetheless, one can fairly enough imagine him, a gilded youth among gilded youths, beginning to learn the graces and vices of the fashionable world as well as polishing his Latin. These graces and vices were to be given further luster at Gray's Inn, where he was admitted in February 1626 / 27. The Inns of Court then provided some legal training for the sons of the landed gentry, but undoubtedly served even more as a clubbish way-station for young men en route to their careers. Devotees of poetry, gambling, and wenching would find congenial companions in the Inns. Suckling's stay at Gray's Inn, however, was a short one.

IV *"the Greatest Gallant . . . and the Greatest Gamester"*

On March 27, 1627, Sir John Suckling the elder died, "worth something in excess of £25,000, possibly as much as £30,000,"[13] a most substantial sum in those days. Undoubtedly something of his father's estimate of his son's character can be seen in the proviso of his will that the lands were to be held in trust until the heir reached the age of twenty-five. It was a most excellent and sensible precaution, but of little use in controlling so determined a spendthrift as the eighteen-year-old John Suckling.

John went to Norwich for his father's funeral and two months later began his travels abroad. It is likely that he joined in May 1627 the cavalry troop of Lord Mountjoy in the expedition to the Island of Rhé, off the port of Rochelle. The campaign, under the command of the Duke of Buckingham, was intended to secure Rhé as an operational base in support of the French Protestants in their stronghold at Rochelle. The English troops were a poor lot; supplies and planning were both in short supply, and the expedition was a total failure. More than half of the English soldiers were lost, the majority through disease.

Suckling's introduction to martial glory, then, was not such as to encourage romantic visions. If he was later to raise his own glorious and fantastical troop of Ruritanian cavalry, there was, nonetheless, little in his experience to encourage fantasies. It is no surprise that about this time references to his gambling begin to appear. One can easily imagine the young man passing the tedious hours of military waiting in tents at cards and dice with his fellow officers and gentlemen volunteers.

The English began their costly retreat from Rhé in October 1628; Suckling's continental adventures, however, were to continue. By November 1629 he was most likely in the Low Countries, for a license to go to Utrecht to serve as volunteers in the troops of the Earl of Wimbledon in the Dutch service was granted to him and to one Colbie on October 22, 1629.[14] A contemporary account lists Suckling's name among those who served with Wimbledon's troops at the siege of Bois-le-duc, but the evidence is inconclusive.[15] The surviving letters of this time point to touring rather than to fighting, but he was not an enthusiastic tourist. To his friend William Wallis he reported, "the Cuntry is stark nought, and yet too good for the inhabitants. . . ." (114)

Another letter to Wallis is equally negative (albeit facetious) in its assessment of the inhabitants of Brussels:

As for their Religion, it is a thing I cannot say much of, as having not yet sufficiently dived into it. Yet as far as I conceive of it, it would suit well enough with us young men. If a man be drunke overnight, it is but Confessing it next morning or when he is sober, and the matter proves not Mortal. To the liing with ones Sister, there is no more required than the telling the truth of it to a ghostly father. And you may jumble as many wenches as you please upon bedds, provided you will but mumble as many *Avemaries* upon beads. (117)

At about the same time he was writing in this fashion to his uncle, Lionel Cranfield, Earl of Middlesex:

Though there be nothing that I can write, that can deserve your Lordships patience in the reading, yet (since the Neglect of my duty cannot but prove a greater sinn then that of being troublesome) the presentation of my devotions shall find I trust though not your acceptation yet your pardon, and the boldness of your humble servant be held excused, if he shall now disturb your greater and better affaires, with a rude relation of the occurences in these parts, which at this present are most of all unworthy your sight, in respect that the preparation unto the warr (the Onely news the season of the yeare affords) are now but meane and poore! (114)

Although the latter is almost a parody of the pompous and unctuous style of the period coming to so tame and flat a conclusion, all that labor to produce a mouse, the passages do serve to remind us of the contrast between the easygoing, fashionable, witty young man on his travels and the dutiful nephew, anxious to send back political news to his influential uncle. The remainder of the letter is a competent job of political reporting; Suckling was, it appears, not entirely just an irresponsible rakehell, but a young man anxious to find a place for himself in the world, a person who wanted to be taken seriously by serious men. A further seriousness may be seen in the fact that he was inscribed in the rolls at Leyden University on 26 February 1629/30.[16]

His study of astrology at Leyden was not of long duration, and despite the indications of a serious side to him, John Aubrey's portrait, based as it is on the information of one of Suckling's good friends, is probably fairly accurate: "He returned to England an extraordinary accomplished Gent., grew famous at Court for his readie sparkling witt; which was envyed, and he was (Sir William Davenant sayd) the Bull that was bayted. He was incomparably readie at repartying, and his Witt most sparkling when most sett-upon and provoked."[17]

Whether his purchase of a knighthood is an indication of seriousness or frivolity is open to question, but in September 1630 he was knighted by King Charles. The sale of honors was a means of replenishing the royal exchequer, and Suckling's knighthood is an indication of the amplitude of his fortune rather than of any intrinsic merits. Still, the glitter of the witty courtier must have been enhanced by the new title.

In 1631 Sir John was again on his travels, this time with the diplomat Sir Henry Vane, who was sent as ambassador extraordinary to King Gustavus Adolphus of Sweden, then campaigning in Germany. The ambassador's party finally reached Gustavus Adolphus's headquarters in Würzburg. Suckling reported to his uncle, the Earl of Middlesex, that the "journey [was] dangerous and troublesome both in respect wee have past through onely the ruines of countryes and also that partyes of horse and foot were every where abroad" (119). The young courtier was in the midst of major events of his time, and in another letter to Middlesex wrote: "I have some things of secret (so great a statesman am I growne on the suddain) which I could wish your Lordship had, but all our lettres goe in great danger of intercepting and there are other respects, greater than that, which makes me not dare to send them but in Cyphre . . ." (124). The letter as a whole is a sober account of military and political matters and reflects Suckling's excitement and interest in being involved in these affairs.

In April 1632 Sir John returned to England carrying dispatches for the court. His report to Sir Henry Vane, a long letter, much of it in code, once more shows the serious side of his nature: "On *Tuesday* I arrived at Court and came soone enough to find the face of it extremely changed, lookinge asquint upon you in *Germany*, as well as upon all us that were sent from thence. The fault at first I layd upon the night and my owne bad eys, but the next day made it cleare and plaine" (126). He is a young man learning the arts of the courtier and diplomat and he is capable of effective political maneuver. The coolness toward Vane and his messenger which he suspected in the evening is confirmed in the morning, "Somethinge coole if not cold!" (126). He delays in making his report to the king, takes soundings with his uncle, the Earl of Middlesex, and with Vane's son, and concludes that the Lord Treasurer needs special courtship:

In the Conclusion I told him, that if there were anythinge in what I had sayd, that could seeme lesse fitt to his Lordship or anythinge besides that his Lordship could thinke more fitt, I stood there ready to be disposd of by him. Upon which he imbraced me, thankt your Lordship more especially for that Addresse, promised to send away presently to you, and wild me to

attend while he came to the king, that he might present me, which he did.
The king was very well pleasd and satisfyed, much better than he was at my
first appeariage. . . . (127)

The letter continues with a thoughtful report of Vane's position in
the court and of the causes of the opposition to him, even to the
gossip of the court ladies: "Then againe the weomen take it ill, that
your son should bee a states-man before theirs, and my Lady
Weston has lett fall in a manner so much to my Lady *Dane*" (128).
The letter is the work of an able and intelligent observer. It is too
easy to write Suckling off as a witty, literate fop.
    Still, these serious aspects of Suckling's character need to be
balanced against Aubrey's observation:

He was the greatest gallant of his time, and the greatest Gamester, both for
Bowling and Cards, so that no Shopkeeper would trust him for 6d, as today,
for instance, he might, by winning, be worth 200 pounds, and the next day
he might not be worth half so much, or perhaps sometimes be *minus nihilo*.
He was one of the best Bowlers of his time in England. He played at Cards
rarely well, and did use to practise by himselfe-a-bed, and there studyed
how the best way of managing the cards could be. His Sisters would come
to the Piccadillo-bowling-green, crying for feare he should loose all their
portions.[18]

The delightfully theatrical picture of Suckling's sisters weeping at
the edge of the green as the wastrel knight bowled away their
marriage portions is undoubtedly Aubreyesque apocrypha, but
Herbert Berry notes in concrete and chilling detail Suckling's growing involvement in gambling and his precarious financial position.
    In 1634 Suckling was twenty-five and came into direct possession
of his inheritance. From now on it is increasingly difficult to make
much of a case for Suckling as a potentially ambitious and sober-
minded young man. In this same year he was involved with a sharp
practicer named Sir John Morley, a figure appropriate to Jonsonian
gulling comedy. Morley, Berry says, managed to borrow £2,600
from Suckling and then persuaded him to play at a dice game called
five and five for the amount of the loan.[19] Suckling lost the £2,600
and an additional £1,200. It is little wonder that we find him about
this time vigorously pursuing an heiress, Anne Willoughby, the
daughter of a wealthy baronet, Sir Henry Willoughby.
    The story of Suckling's unsuccessful attempt to procure a rich
bride reads like the scenario of a Caroline comedy of intrigue. Ser-

vants were corrupted; the support of the king was enlisted; Anne
Willoughby was persuaded to initial a document saying she would
like to marry Suckling. Sir Henry Willoughby wrote angrily to King
Charles himself complaining bitterly (and justifiably) of Sir John:

> His proud and disdainfull Carriage towards me in my owne per-
> son. . . . His sending a Challenge . . . to fight in Duell with my
> brother. . . . His being as I am crediblye informed noe gentleman by
> birth, otherwise than by being sonne to one that from a most obscure and
> lowe beginning had the honour to be imployed in your Majesties service.
> His haveing a Meane state in noe degree proportionable to the fortune my
> daughter may bring with her, which alsoe I understand is much incumbred,
> and weakened by his owne Rioutous liveing, his unlimited gameing and
> profuse expences which with a much greater estate then all mine is in
> probabilitye likelye to last but a small time. Finallye his haveing so un-
> luckye a Reputation with all persons of honour that knowe him, that that
> woman must be unfortunate that shall be his wife. (198 - 99)

Suckling's life seems to have been imitating art with a vengeance.
In proper comic fashion this story was concluded with a brawl.

Willoughby decided his daughter was to marry Sir John Digby,
the brother of Sir Kenelm Digby, the famous pirate, alchemist, and
scholar. In November of 1634 Digby cudgeled Sucking, who (dis-
creetly enough, for Digby was a noted swordsman) took the beating
without drawing his sword. Later in the month Suckling avenged
himself by assaulting Digby and some friends outside Blackfriars
Theater with a gang of sixteen men. Suckling wore a rapier-proof
vest, but one of his men was killed. Suckling's reputation, already so
dubious in the eyes of respectable folk like Sir Henry Willoughby,
was not helped by this affair. "Mr. Snowdon," wrote John Aubrey,
"tells me that after Sir John's . . . Quarrel with Sir John Digby . . .
'twas strange to see the envie and ill-nature of people to trample,
and Scoffe at, and deject one in disgrace. . . ."[20] That reputation
looks even worse when one considers the bragging note he wrote Sir
Kenelm Digby regarding the incident: "The common report tells
mee, that you have bine a large talker in my affaires; doing
becomes a man better; Know then (Sir) that I have switcht your
brother, and hee hath run away upon it; You have profest to maintaine your Brothers actions, and I, to maintaine myne owne; And I
may thinke, til I know the contrarie, You dare not question any of
them" (130). The letter is the only account in which Suckling
appears as a victor in the Digby affair. Disgraceful and childish it all

is, but it serves as a reminder that the elegant, silken courtier painted by Sir Anthony Van Dyck was not just capable of a street brawl but of mendaciously boasting about it. Sir Henry Willoughby was surely well advised to protect his daughter and his duckets from such a suitor.

The most cheering note in Suckling's life at this time is perhaps the £1,200 he seems to have won from Lord Dunluce at ninepins. It is not, admittedly, a very poetic note. But gambling, roistering, and the cheerful debauchery of the courtly gallant one guesses occupied Suckling's attention more fully than poetry. By this time he had sold all the estates inherited from his father, amounting to a most impressive figure of some £7,381.[21] To spend money on that scale, even in the seventeenth century, is the achievement of no mere amateur wastrel.

V *The Writing Gambler*

Nevertheless, "Upon the first sight of my Lady Seimor," the witty parody of Jonson in "A Song to a Lute," and "Upon My Lady Carliles walking in Hampton-Court garden," all three of which can be dated before 1633, clearly demonstrate Suckling's artistic achievement. The poems of this period are few in number, but well wrought. "Why so pale and wan fond Lover," which Suckling's editor, Thomas Clayton, places with those poems written between 1632 and 1637, could have been written by a rakehell with a hangover, but a hungover rakehell with a poetic facility that comes only through artistic discipline and continued practice. It is not the sort of poem one just "throws off."

Still, it is in 1637 and 1638 that Suckling's literary work is most visible. At this time he must have been devoting a considerable portion of his energies to writing. After practicing with the unfinished play, *The Sad One*, he went on to write *Aglaura*, which was produced at court in the Christmas season of 1637. According to one letter writer, "Sutlin's Play cost three or four hundred Pounds setting out, eight or ten suits of new Cloaths he gave the Players; an unheard of Prodigality."[22] Suckling set out to make a dramatic splash and did so. The elaborate public-relations operation extended to a handsome manuscript copy of the play presented to the king and to its publication, not in humble quarto, but in magnificent, wide-margined folio. The play, with its two last acts—one tragic and the other tragicomic—and its elaborate and costly mounting inspired considerable comment, some of it, not surprisingly, satiric. The professional playwright Richard Brome was sufficiently annoyed with the elegant amateur to take after Suckling with forty-two lines of verse. The margins of the folio particularly irritated Brome:

> When I saw so much white, I did begin
> To think *Aglaura* either did lye in,
> Or else did Penance, never did I see
> (Unlesse in Bills dash'd in the Chancery)
> So little in so much, as if the feet
> Of Poetry, like Law, were sold by th' sheet.[23]

If Sir John Suckling has any poems which can be called major, they also belong to this period. "The Wits," or by its variant and more familiar title, "A Sessions of the Poets," was written in the summer of 1637, and the king had it sung to him in the autumn of that year. In this mock-literary contest for Apollo's reward Suckling modestly denies his poetic interests, claiming, "He loved not the Muses so well as his sport," but the verses confirm the sense of Suckling's own self-conception of himself as a poet in a distinct and specific poetic milieu. The second major poem of this period is "A Ballade. Upon a Wedding," celebrating the marriage of John Lord Lovelace and Lady Anne Wentworth in July 1638.

There is no difficulty in associating *Aglaura*, "The Wits," and "A Ballade. Upon a Wedding" together and with their creator. But that Sir John Suckling would ever write *An Account of Religion by Reason* might seem surprising, yet the times were full of surprises. The essay was written while Sir John was on an excursion to Bath in August and September 1637 with his friends Jack Young and Sir William Davenant. Aubrey's gossipy account is too delightful a yarn and too lively an insight into Suckling's world to ignore:

Sir John came like a young Prince for all manner of Equipage and convenience, and Sir W. Davenant told me that he had a Cart-load of Bookes carried downe; and 'twas there, at Bath that he writt the little Tract in his Booke about Socinianism. 'Twas as pleasant a journey as ever men had; in the height of a long Peace and luxury, and in the Venison Season. The second night they lay at Marlborough, and walking on the delicate fine downes at the Backside of the Towne, whilest supper was making ready, the maydes were drying of cloathes on the bushes. Jack Young had espied a very pretty young Girle, and had gott her consent for an assignation, which

was about midnight, which they happened to overheare on the other side of
the hedge, and were resolved to frustrate his designe. They were wont
every night to play at cards after supper a good while: but Jack Young
pretended wearinesse, etc., and must needes goe to Bed, not to be perswaded by any meanes to the contrary. They had their landlady at supper with
them; said they to her, Observe this poor Gentleman, how he yawnes: now
is his mad fit comeing uppon him. We beseech you that you make fast his
doores, and gett somebody to watch and looke to him, for about midnight
he will fall to be most outragious. Gett the Hostler, or some strong fellow,
to stay-up, and we will well content him, for he is our worthy friend, and a
very honest Gent., only, perhaps twice in a yeare he falls into these fitts.

Jack Young slept not, but was ready to goe out as the clock struck to the
houre of appointment, and then going to open the Dore he was disappointed, knocks, bounces, stampes, calls, *Tapster! Chamberlayne! Hostler!*
sweares and curses dreadfully; nobody would come to him. Sir John and W.
Davenant were expectant all this time, and ready to dye with laughter. I
know not how he happened to gett open the Dore, and was comeing downe
stayres. The Hostler, a huge lusty fellow, fell uppon him, and held him, and
cryed, Good Sir, take God in your mind, you shall not goe out to destroy
your selfe. J. Young struggled and strived, insomuch that at last he was
quite spent and dispirited, and was faine to goe to bed to rest himselfe.

In the morning the Landlady of the House came to see how he did, and
brought him a Cawdle; Oh, Sir, sayd she, You had a heavy fitt last night;
pray, Sir, be pleased to take some of this to comfort your heart. Jack Young
thought the woman had been mad, and being exceedingly vexed, flirted the
porrenger of Cawdle in her face. The next day his Camerades told him all
the plott, how they crosse-bitt him.[24]

The association of this story with *An Account of Religion by Reason*
is another reminder of the complexity of Suckling's character. Or
perhaps it is better to see the juxtaposition as demonstration of the
degree to which Suckling satisfied the Renaissance expectations of
gentlemanly wholeness. He could take time off from his play to be
serious; the boon companion could and did talk and write
philosophy.

At any rate, by 1638 Sir John had established himself as
something more than a courtier and gambler. The dedications of
works by Wye Saltonstall and Thomas Nabbes to Suckling suggest
the critic as well as patron. That he would attract dedications at this
time might also, however, be a result of increased courtly influence
and prestige. He was appointed a Gentleman of the Privy Chamber
Extraordinary on November 20, 1638; one had to pay a fee for the
post, but most court honors were bought and sold. Perhaps even

more important is the fact that he was granted a pension from the king. The date of the grant is not known, but its existence is sure since Parliament officially took it away when Suckling fled to France.[25] A letter from Lord Dudley North accompanying a copy of his verses, "Corona," asks from Suckling "friendly correction," an even more tangible indication of Sir John's literary status.

To this picture of literary productivity and growing favor in the court can be added Sir John's possibly serious romantic involvement with the young woman to whom he gave the romantic sobriquet "Aglaura." The primary candidates for the title are his cousin, Mary Cranfield, and Mary Bulkeley, the eldest daughter of a prosperous family who lived in Wales at Baron Hill, Beaumaris, Anglesey.[26] Although Suckling may well have been genuinely attached to his cousin, Mary Bulkeley has best claim to the title. Mary Cranfield died in 1635, and, as Professor Clayton has pointed out, her relationship with Suckling seems to have cooled by 1633.[27] Assuming that Mary Bulkeley and Aglaura are the same, about all that can be said with any certainty about this romance is that Suckling appears to have made a serious attempt to marry her. The existing letters and *Aglaura* itself give no certain clue to his real feelings toward the lady. She is the "Dear Princesse" of the letters, but the letters associated with her reveal more of Suckling's wit than his emotions: "Why should I not come my self? Those Tyrants, businesse, honour, and necessity, what have they to do with you and I? Why should we not do Loves commands before theirs whose Soveraignty is but usurped upon us? Shall we not smell to Roses 'cause others do look on? or gather them, 'cause there are prickles, and something that would hinder us?" (138). Whatever Suckling may have really felt about Aglaura, marriage eluded him. At the end of September 1639 he was writing the Earl of Middlesex, "I intend to kisse Mrs. *Buckleys* hands" (149), but she would shortly marry another.

VI *Captain Suckling*

The failure of Suckling's courtship is perhaps made more poignant by the fact that the spring and summer of 1639 see the poet in full dress as Cavalier, but a Cavalier in a seriocomic campaign which can be viewed as the beginning of the end of the Cavalier world. In 1639 King Charles responded to Scottish opposition to the episcopacy by raising an army and marching north. The First

Bishops' War was scarcely a war and ended with the high-sounding, but inconclusive, Treaty of Berwick.

Suckling's part in this venture was to raise his famous cavalry troop "of 100 very handsome young proper men, whom he clad in white doubletts and scarlett breeches, and scarlet Coates, hatts, and feathers, well horsed and armed."[28] It must have been, as Aubrey says, "one of the finest sights in those days." The splendid troop rode north in its finery, weapons glinting in the sun, feathers waving, spurs jingling, and took part in the general debacle. In the only event approaching combat, near Kelso, the English under Lord Holland, were martialed before the Scots but took a careful look at the numerically superior enemy and withdrew. In a letter to his uncle, the Earl of Middlesex, Suckling reported: "Our horse are much harast by Continuall Alarums and hard marches, and our men, manie sick of Loosnesses and Plurisies, which wee ascribe to their violent drinking of *Twede* water that daie wee went to *Kelsey*. The first of the diseases I suffered my share in through the same cause" (146).

That the shimmering troop of silken Cavaliers should finish the glorious campaign in ignominious retreat and wracked by dysentery is a sadly prophetic commentary on the royalist cause. Suckling's flashy gesture became, of course, the object of considerable ridicule and lampoon followed lampoon.

> When he came to the Camp, he was in a damp
>   To see the *Scots* in sight a,
> And all his brave Troops like so many droops,
>   To fight they had no heart a.
> And when the Allarme cal'd all to arme,
>   Sir *John* he went to shite a.[29]

The lines have a certain authenticity, but the joke is lessened when we recall that the poet and playwright, Shackerley Marmion, a member of Suckling's troop, may have died as a result of dysentery contracted during the First Bishops' War. Other literary figures on the same campaign were William Davenant, Thomas Carew, and Richard Lovelace. King Charles, at least, did not go to war without regard for the Muse.

Suckling's attitude toward the Scots is seen in a political tract in letter form, "An Answer to a Gentleman in Norfolk that sent to enquire after the Scotish business." He is as intransigent and arrogant as his uniforms were gaudy: "If it be Liberty of Conscience they ask, 'tis a foolish request, since they have it already, and must have it in despight of power. . . . If the exercise of Liberty, 'tis dangerous . . ." (143). The letter shows more wit and traditional English antipathy to the Scots than political awareness, but that is a characteristic of the Cavalier. This letter was apparently written during the march to the north.

Another letter written a few days before the retreat at Kelso gives further emphasis to Suckling's attitude at the start of the First Bishops' War. "So (Sir) you may now imagine us walking up and down the banks of the *Tweed* like Tower-Lyons in their Cages, leaving the people to think what we would do if we were let loose. The Enemy is not yet much visible, (It may be it is the fault of the Climate, which brings men as slowly forwards as Plants:) But it gives us fears that the Men of Peace will draw all this to a dumb shew, and so destroy a handsom opportunity which was now offered, of producing glorious matter for future Chronicle" (144). The matter for future chronicle, of course, was the grandiloquently named, face-saving Treaty of Berwick, and an inglorious retreat. Suckling and his troops, their fine uniforms stained and torn, their feathers drooping, must have returned to London in a melancholy frame of mind.

In September Suckling may have been on his way "to kisse Mrs. Buckleys hand"; but if he did so, it was for the last time. In October of 1639 he was writing a decidedly cheery and hard-boiled letter of consolation to his sister Martha, whose disagreeable husband, Sir George Southcot, had committed suicide. The rare view of Suckling as a solicitous brother gives way again to the public figure. The continued intransigence of the Scots led King Charles to raise another army for what was to become known as the Second Bishops' War. In February 1640 Suckling was commissioned "captain of a troop of carabineers,"[30] but he was also busily trying to sell the government the weapons he had acquired for his troop in the First Bishops' War. Financial exigencies were clearly influencing Sir John's loyalty and his views on the value of gesture.

His return to military life was delayed, moreover, by political activity—his brief membership in the so-called Short Parliament. King Charles called Parliament into session on April 13, 1640. On April 30 Suckling took his seat as member for Bramber, Sussex. The election was contested and there were charges of bribery and threats. Whatever the case, Suckling was a Member of Parliament

for only five days, for the king adjourned the Parliament on May 5.
Suckling was then able to join the English army in the north in time
to participate in its retreat. The Second Bishops' War ended with
the defeat of the English at Newburn Ford, near Newcastle, on
August 28. Suckling is rumored to have lost some horses and his
coach with clothes and money in it. But all that is certain is that he
shared in the general English humiliation.

VII   Plot, Flight, and Suicide

His ardor for the king's cause, however, was not extinguished by
defeat and an epistolary tract *To Mr. Henry German. In the Beginning of Parliament, 1640* opens with the straightforward assertion,
"That it is fitt for the Kinge to doe somethinge extraordinary att
this present, is not onely the opinion of the wise, but their expectation" (163). Sir John's commitment to action and to the king
would shortly lead to his exile and death.

Meanwhile, however, he was at work on *The Goblins*, a play concerned with "things that ne're were, nor are, nor ne're will be."[31] In
"On New-years day 1640. To the King" Suckling could pray:

> May no ill vapour cloud the skie,
> Bold storms invade the Soveraigntie,
> But gales of joy, so fresh, so high,
> That You may think Heav'n sent to try this year
> What sayl, or burthen, a Kings mind could bear.
>
> (85, 11 - 15)

But in the early part of 1641 he was writing *Brennoralt*. The play os-
tensibly deals with Lithuanians revolting against the Poles;
however, the parallels to the military and political situation in Britain were clear enough. While Suckling was creating a stage echo of
Britain's problems he was becoming involved with, as C. V.
Wedgwood describes it, one of the groups "who moved in and out
of each other's lodgings of an evening to take sack and tobacco, met
in the Westminster taverns, and attended—some of them—the
Queen's drawing-room. Their business in politics and at Court had
nothing to do with the King's policy of moderation and patient
waiting. They represented the beginnings of a new striking force, a
new extremism of which the Queen was the moving spirit."[32] The
result of these meetings was the Army Plot conceived by the

Queen's Master of the Horse, Henry Jermyn, Suckling, and his friend and fellow poet, Sir William Davenant. They included in the plot Colonel George Goring, a sometime gambling friend of Sir John and the commander of the fortress at Portsmouth. "To the Couple! to the Couple! th'are Divine."[33] ends Lovelace's "Sonnet" to this gentleman who was not so divine that he hesitated to betray Suckling and the other conspirators when he was convinced that the plot would fail. The intent of the plan was to use the army to gain control of Parliament and thus restore the king to a position of strength. A letter of Suckling's to the Earl of Newcastle written on January 8, 1641 suggests an attempt to draw the earl into the plot, an attempt no more successful than the Army Plot itself.

At the end of April Sir John was raising troops and was reported meeting with some sixty armed men in the White Horse Tavern. The House of Commons examined Suckling on May 3 and he testified that he was recruiting soldiers for service in Portugal. But, of course, the troops were a part of the Army Plot and the plan to rescue the Earl of Strafford from the Tower. The House of Commons had already passed a Bill of Attainder against Strafford. The revelation of the Army Plot undoubtedly pushed the House of Lords to its decision to pass the bill as well.

At any rate, the plot being revealed, Suckling and Jermyn did not choose to testify before Parliament again but, recognizing their heads were in danger, fled to Portsmouth and thence to Dieppe on the royal pinnace *Roebuck*, on Thursday, May 6.[34] Suckling reached Paris on Friday, May 14, but after that nothing is certain. The specific time and mode of his death is vague. He was most probably dead by the end of 1641. Aubrey is mistaken as to the date of his death, but his account is no doubt as true as any we shall have:

He went into France, where after sometime, being come to the bottome of his Found [i.e., broke and hopeless], reflecting on the miserable and despicable condition he should be reduced to, having nothing left to maintaine him, he (having a convenience for that purpose, lyeing at an apothecarie's house in Paris) tooke poyson, which killed him miserably with vomiting.[35]

The Earl of Strafford he had tried to save was dead on the scaffold, betrayed by the king they had both served. Had Sir John returned to England, he would have been tried and undoubtedly convicted of high treason. What lay ahead was lonely and impoverished exile. He saw no chance of recovery; the gambler knew the game was over.

The tragic brevity of Suckling's life stands in sharp contrast to the polish, to the apparent ease and gaiety of his writing. But in that contrast one can find something of the note of desperation which lurks behind the facade. The silken courtier died miserably, wracked with vomiting, among strangers. Yet out of that life came a body of work that still demands our attention for its steadfast artifice, its humor, the play of its wit, and its design against the chaos.

CHAPTER 2

The Prose: A Bright and Elegant Surface

I Letters and the Hidden Self

S UCKLING'S prose is limited in quantity, consisting of
fifty-four or fifty-five letters, depending on one's view of a
doubtful one,[1] and An Account of Religion by Reason, a short essay.
From so small a sample of his prose one might be hesitant to conclude with Tucker Brooke, "There is hardly a purer English style in
the seventeenth century than Suckling's, and there are few better
personal letters of the period than [those] of his that have been
preserved."[2] But it would be impossible not to agree that the style is
indeed notable and the letters of considerable interest. Moreover,
the prose, apart from its intrinsic merits, can be used to provide in-
sights into Suckling not to be found in the poetry or plays. In addition, and more importantly, through the art of the letters one can
more clearly perceive the art of the poetry and certain literary
values and assumptions of the period.

The letters can be divided into four main groups: (1) letters of a
personal nature, including both kinds of courtship—that is, love and
manners; (2) witty letters and letters belonging to epistolary genres;
(3) serious letters concerning politics and war; and finally, (4) family
letters. The seventeen identified correspondents, including his
sister, Lady Southcot; his uncle, the Earl of Middlesex; Mary
Bulkeley, the probable Aglaura; his friend Thomas Carew; his
enemy Sir Kenelm Digby, give us some sense of Suckling's social
world. However, it is difficult to discover in the letters what might
be called his private world or something of the actual self, the
"real" John Suckling.

Of course, one letter-writer can present a variety of "selves" in a
number of letters. Moods, purposes, and recipients will all affect the

33

tone and pose of a letter. The problem is compounded in the seventeenth century by the development of the familiar letter as a genre itself. On the continent and in English translation as well the *Lettres* of Jean Louis Guez de Balzac, published in 1624 and translated into English in 1634 and 1638, enjoyed wide popularity and supplied Suckling with a phrase or idea now and then. In England the most famous example of the familiar letter was James Howell's *Epistolae Ho-Elianae*, which appeared after Suckling's death, but an earlier and popular exemplar, one which Suckling knew and used, was Nicholas Breton's *Post With a Mad Packet of Letters*, first published in 1602. In these works the letter becomes a branch of the essay. The relationship of the writer to the letter is as personal or impersonal as it is to the essay, which is simply to say that it is as erroneous to expect personal revelation from some seventeenth-century letters as it is to expect it from poems of the period. The letter can be as crafted, artificial, and uninhabited as any song to Delia, Celia, or Aglaura.

Oddly enough the most personal of Suckling's letters are those having to do with serious matters, letters which can almost be called business letters. These letters, half of them written to the Earl of Middlesex, were not published in either *Fragmenta Aurea* or *The Last Remains* and are more distinctly private than the published letters. In the letters concerning serious business, at any rate, one finds less concern with craftsmanship and less posing. If the subject matter demands a degree of impersonality, these letters plus *An Account of Religion by Reason* at the very least provide us with a glimpse of another, the least familiar, facet of Suckling's character and work.

II *War, Politics, and the Serious World*

This group includes eighteen letters, addressed to five identified persons: his uncle the Earl of Middlesex, Viscount Conway, the Earl of Newcastle, Sir Henry Vane, and Henry Jermyn. The letter to Jermyn, a favorite of Queen Henrietta Maria, is a political tract, as are three other letters addressed to unknown or imaginary correspondents. Half of the letters are to Suckling's uncle. The letters fall into two periods, those written in 1630 - 32 when Suckling was in Europe, part of the time in the party of Sir Henry Vane, ambassador to King Gustavus Adolphus of Sweden; the other group begins six years later, and the letters concern the developing civil war in Britain.

It is in the first group of letters in particular that one sees the serious and ambitious side of Suckling not apparent in his poetry. The letters to his uncle are straightforward, businesslike reports on the military situation in Germany. Occasionally a vivid detail will charge a letter with immediacy, ". . . the Castle by assault he took the seventh of *October*, where the Souldier found such pillage, that it is ordinary for the lower ranke of them now to loose 300 Duckets upon a drums head" (120). But the reader is less struck by felicities of style than by the sense of the writer as a potentially serious and ambitious young man, caught up in the excitement of great events and anxious to play a significant part in the world of affairs.

In the letter just cited, written to the Earl of Middlesex from Würzburg on November 9, 1631, he mentions dining with James, third Marquis and first Duke of Hamilton, who was serving with the army of the Swedish King Gustavus Adolphus:

Last night I went to supp with my Lord Marquis and wishing that some occasion might present it self wherein I might serve him, he was pleasd to tell me, that he was now going to beseidge *Magdeburg*, and that his army would be there before him. He is between 7 and 8000 strong but they are most of them *Duch* and given him by the king, for his owne are al dead of the plage to 1200. The king esteems much of him, and the Souldier honors him, and he himself takes al the ways to become a brave souldier, and to doe some act worthy of himselfe. (120)

If the reader fails to catch the young Suckling's excitement and his attraction here to the values Hamilton represents, one can't miss these feelings in the next sentence; for the description of Hamilton becomes the occasion for an appeal to Middlesex, in retirement since his impeachment in 1624, to return to active public life: "While all the world is thus in action, pardon me (my Lord) if I must hope your Lordshipp will not long be idle. . . . The Christian world never more needing able men then at this present" (120).

Suckling's late father had been, after all, a member of the Privy Council and Comptroller of the King's Household, with all the avenues for advancing a son such a post possessed. His uncle had been, until his impeachment, Lord Treasurer of England. How exasperating it must have been for so lively a young man to have so potentially influential a relative inactive. The intensity of Suckling's hope that his uncle might reenter political life is seen again in letter 15. The letter is uncertain both as to date and addressee, but the subject matter and relation to other letters make the argument that it was written in November 1631 and addressed to the Earl of Middlesex most convincing.[3]

The letter is an epistolary "Character" urging, like the earlier letter, a return to active involvement in affairs: "When I consider you look (to me) like—I cannot but think it as odd a thing, as if I should see *Van Dike* with all his fine colours and Pensills about him, his Frame, and right Light, and everything in order, and yet his hands tyed behind him: and your Lordship must excuse me if upon it I be as bold" (121). The comparison of Middlesex with the brilliant painter is deftly done and effectively removes any sugges-tion of impertinence in the proposal. Suckling goes on to argue that both honor and wealth urge active engagement in the political world. The most interesting portion of the letter, however, is found in the high-flown praise of the court of King Charles:

The little word behind the back, the undoing whisper, which like pulling of a sheatrope at Sea, slackens the sail, and makes the gallantest ship stand still; that that heretofore made the faulty and innocent alike guilty, is a thing, I beleeve, now so forgot, or at least so unpractiz'd, that those that are the worst, have leisure to grow good, before any will take notice they have been otherwise, or at least divulge it. . . . The very women have suffered reformation, and wear through the whole Court their faces as little dis-guised now, as an honest mans actions should be, and if there be any have suffer'd themselves to be gained by their servants, their ignorance of what they granted may well excuse them for the shame of what they did. So that it is more then possible to be great and good. . . . (122 - 23)

On May 2, 1632, on the other hand, Suckling was writing to Sir Henry Vane, in a letter discussed in the first chapter, a report of the reception he received when he brought Vane's dispatches from Ger-many to court, "The pacquett to my Lord Treasurer I presented first and the takinge of *Donawart*, who both to the bearer and the news seemd alike indifferent! Somethinge coole if not cold! Perchance his garb" (126). The letter then details the intricacies of court suspicions and rivalries, including "The disposall of the Coferers place [which] makes the world thinke, that there is some staggering in the friendship betwixt my Lord Treasurer and you . . ." (127) and the maneuverings necessary to get a hearing for Vane's reports. The realism of this account contrasts sharply with the idealistic (despite the inevitable gibe in passing at court ladies) picture of the "reformed" court presented to the Earl of Middlesex. The contrast underlines the distinctly literary aspect of even some of the "business letters" and the ease with which the Caroline writer is able to move from an idealistic, imaginary, artistically created vision of the court to a perfectly realistic, straightforward description of it. The astounding facility and rapidity of this shift from the crafted, artificial world of idealized court to a real, conniving, infighting, everyday court is symptomatic of the period, and a theme which will be amplified later. For the moment one may simply note that the shift of worlds forms the basis of the delightful poem "Upon my Lady Carliles walking in Hampton-Court garden." Before leaving the letter to Vane it should be stated that it reinforces the view of Suckling as a competent and perceptive political operative. The letter is well constructed, lively, and acute. One comes from a reading of it impressed by Suckling's ability and by his competent service to Vane—surely exactly the impression the writer strove to create.

After this letter there is a six-year jump in the public-affairs letters. The subject matter moves from European wars to the growing civil strife in England and Scotland. The author is no longer a youth with a career to make, but a mature man of thirty, for better or worse established, as much as he ever would be, in life.

This second group opens with a pair of letters purporting to be an exchange between a "London alderman" and a "Scottish Lord." Both are political pieces written for propagandistic purposes. Neither letter is especially noteworthy, but both are mildly amusing. The tone of the pair can be seen in the concluding thrust at the London citizen in the London alderman's letter, "I therefore desire your Lordship to send me word in what state things stand there, that I may know of which side to be . . ." (141). The irony increases in the answering letter from the Scottish Lord, who professes great surprise that he and his fellows should be called "Rebels, when none are more his Majesties most humble Subjects than we, as in the front of our Petitions and Messages most plainly appears . . ." (141). Suckling's technique in this pair of letters is to attack both the rebellious Scots and their London sympathizers through the creation of two unattractive spokesmen. Both are hypocrites, and differences dividing the kingdom are the consequence of the self-seeking unruliness of such rogues as these. Suck-

ling can hardly have hoped to persuade anyone to the king's side by
this method, but persuasion is not much found in his political
writing.

The epistolary tract of April 1639, "An Answer to a Gentleman in
Norfolk that sent to enquire after the Scotish business," exemplifies
Suckling's basic intransigence. It is worth examining in some detail
simply for its polemical skill. The letter may have been written to
Suckling's uncle, Charles Suckling of Woodton, Norfolk, but it is
very likely that the Gentleman in Norfolk is a convenient fiction.
The letter, an exercise in loyalist propaganda, was probably written
from York when Suckling was on his way to Scotland and the First
Bishops' War.

It begins with a statement of purpose which declares his an-
noyance with timid and ambiguous positions: "That you may
receive an account of the Scotish businesse, and why there hath
been such irresolution and alteration about the Levies lately; it is fit
you know that this Northern storm (like a new Disease) hath so far
pos'd the Doctors of State, that as yet they have not given it a
name; though perchance they all firmly believe it to be
Rebellion: . . ." (142). The complexity of the Scottish situation, he
continues, developing a vivid image, leads people to think of it
much as they do the moon, "the simpler think it no bigger then a
Bushel, and some (too wise) imagine it a vast World, with strange
things undiscovered in it . . ." (143). The comparison then leads to
a central assertion: "I confess I know not how to meet it in the middle, or set it right, nor do I think you have: since I should believe
the question to be rather *A King or no King*, then *A Bishop or no
Bishop*" (143). The attitude, then, is one of irreconcilable opposites.
Given that view, the letter moves with its own logic in a series of increasingly strong attacks. There is no argument here; for Suckling
there was nothing to argue.

The religious issue he considers totally spurious, a mask for
rebellion, "for Rebellion it self is so ugly, that did it not put on the
vizard of Religion, it would fright rather then draw people to
it . . ." (143). Nor can they claim freedom of thought as a cause
Suckling airily declares: "If it be Liberty of Conscience they ask, 'tis
a foolish request, since they have it already, and must have it in
despight of power . . ." (143). This can only be called a very
cavalier dismissal. The next step is *ad hominem* with a brilliant and
nasty thrust at the Scots' military leader, Sir Alexander Leslie, who
had served with the armies of the King of Sweden for thirty years:

"*Lesly* himself (if his story were search'd) would certainly be found one, who because he could not live well here, took up a trade of killing men abroad, and now is return'd for Christ's sake to kill men at home" (143 - 44). It would be cheap enough if it weren't so well sneered a sneer. The famous general is reduced to a mere mercenary, a military tradesman and a religious hypocrite. Suckling ends the letter with a final slur, that the Scots simply want more attention from the king and that Scotland (as Dr. Samuel Johnson held a century later) is a wilderness in contrast to the English Eden, "The great and wise Husbandman hath placed the Beasts in the Outfields, and they would break hedges to come into the Garden" (144). It is all supremely superior; the challenge to the royal authority, the questions of church governance do not even deserve argument. Again, one can't help but be impressed by the totality of the pose, by the creation of the languidly superior Cavalier who can so easily and with such artful contempt dismiss the major political-religious questions of the day. Against the cavalier pose may be set the bitter reality of the ignominious nonbattle at Kelso described in a letter to the Earl of Middlesex on June 6, 1639: "And now the word was given to Charg; but by this Time wee discovered dust, and out of that dust grew a greater bodie then all the right and left hand forces were together. It was now time to think of Retreat. . . . Our horse are much harast by Continuall Alarums and hard marches, and our men, many sick of Loosnesses and Plurisies . . ." (145 - 46).

The last major political letter to be considered here is that "To Mr. Henry German, In the Beginning of Parliament, 1640." This tract marks the beginning of Suckling's active participation in the debates and plot that ended with his escape to France. However, the letter to Jermyn, is measured, temperate, and to a large degree a statesmanlike document. In the opening Suckling urges that the king must now act: "That it is fitt for the Kinge to doe somethinge extraordinary att this present, is not only the opinion of the wise, but their expectation. . . . To lie still now would att the best shewe but a calmnes of minde, not a magnanimitie . . ." (163). The balanced stateliness and the forcefulness of the lines just quoted are characteristic of the whole letter. The question of action leads naturally to the specific course of action and to the nature of advice given the king. Suckling's perception here is sound and wittily and gracefully expressed: "Then in the Court they give much

Counsell, as they beleive the King inclyn'd, determine of his good
by his desires, which is a kinde of Settinge the Sun by the Diall,
Interest that cannot erre, by Passions which may" (163).

The interest of the king, he goes on to argue, is "union with his
people," while the two main concerns of the people are religion and
justice. The logic of the argument is that the king must respond in a
real way to his own interests and to those of his people. The striking
aspect of Suckling's thought here is that he has reduced the great
questions of the period to pragmatic basics. He is not concerned
with the details of religion and justice, but with the fact that the
king, needing the loyal support of the people, must respond to their
concerns, and indeed must do more than respond: "It will not bee
enough for the King to doe what they desire, but hee must doe
something more. I meane by doing more, doing something of his
owne: as throwing away things they call not for, or giving things
they expected not" (165). It is rather surprising to hear a man one
thinks of as a kind of arch-Cavalier arguing so pragmatically and
arguing for what would be in modern terms a calculated appeal to
the electorate.

The attitude might be described as cynical by some, but others
would see it as something more than practical, as a natural outcome
of a bent of mind inclined to look beyond the abstractions to the es-
sences. At any rate, the position here described is not at odds with
the thinking that prompted *An Account of Religion by Reason*, as
shall be seen later. The following assertion shows more of Suckling's
practical, realistic outlook: "For the People are naturally not
valiant, and not much Cavaleir. Nowe it is the nature of Cowards to
hurt, when they can receive none: They will not bee content (while
they feare, and have the upper hand) to fetter onely royaltie, but
perchance (as timorous Spirritts use) will not thinke themselves safe,
whiles that is att all, and possibly this may bee the present state of
things" (165).

If one objects to the superior attitude toward the "people,"
Cromwell's men gave adequate refutation to the view; more importantly, it is evident Suckling was prophetically correct as to the consequences of a royal attitude which ignored the popular will. His
practicality here contrasts interestingly with traditional ideality or
court artificiality in the next paragraph. The queen, he says, must
be involved in any action and must support it. Indeed, the direction
of the letter to Jermyn indicates that Suckling's concern is in great
measure with the queen and the extremist position of Henrietta
Maria and her party. The queen must join so that the royal cause be

totally united; then Suckling turns from the day to day argument and language to court argument and the language of courtship:

And to invite her, shee is to consider with herselfe, whether such great vertues and eminent Excellencies (though they bee highly admir'd and valued
by those that know her and are about her) ought to rest satisfied with so
narrowe a payment, as the estimation of a few: and whether it bee not more
proper for a great Queen to arrive att universall honor, and love, than
private esteeme and value. Then how becomeing a worke for the
sweetnesse and softnesse of her Sex is composing differences, and uniting
hearts; and how proper for a Queene, reconciling King and people. (165 -
66)

The language of this indirect appeal to Henrietta Maria takes us
back to the graceful artifices of the court, the world of

> Awake (great Sir) the Sun shines heer,
> Gives all Your Subjects a New-year,
> Onely we stay till You appear,
> For thus by us Your Power is understood:
> He may make fair days, You must make them good.
> (84, 1 - 5)

But the context for the artifice is a hardheaded political tract.

This hardheaded expediency is even more tellingly revealed in
Suckling's advice concerning the king's loyal ministers who in-
curred the displeasure of his opponents. Although he says "I shall
rather propound something about it, than resolve it" (166), his position is clearly that the ministers must be abandoned because the
smaller must be sacrificed to the greater good. If the ministers could
be saved, they would be ineffective because of their unpopularity;
the king really can't save them until he has the power to do so; to
attempt to save them may result in the loss of that power, that is,
the fight might result in the king's downfall. Again, Suckling's advice is sound and undogmatic. The essay concludes with a prayer
which underlines the basic pragmatism of his position:

That the King bee neither too insensible, of what is without him, nor too
resolv'd from what is within him. To bee sicke in a dangerous sicknesse,
and finde noe paine, cannot bee but with losse of understanding. 'Tis an
Aphorisme of *Hippocrates:* And on the other side, *Opiniastrie* is a sullen
Porter and (as it was wittily said of *Constancie*) shutts out oftentymes better
things, than it letts in. (167)

Reading this we know why Suckling could not have written with
Lovelace:

> I could not love thee, dear, so much,
> Lov'd I not Honour more.

And we can understand more readily the dryness, the unlyrical
edge, the just barely hidden melancholy that lurks beneath the
bright surface of much of his poetry. He is not a man for doctrinaire
abstractions. The silken courtier with his glamorous hundred horse,
the pensive and dreamy gentleman of the Van Dyck portrait, lean-
ing against a rock, holding his folio of Shakespeare open to *Hamlet*,
remains, whatever the pose, the gambler who sees the options as
win or lose. The keenness of mind, the clarity and brilliance of style
in these letters concerning practical matters lead one to conclude
that Suckling's Hamlet was not a dreamy, indecisive prince, but the
man of action, the soldier and administrator perceived by Horatio
and Fortinbras. At all events, the least one can conclude is that
Suckling presents a variety of surfaces and more complexity than
might be expected. That complexity is underscored by the last prose
work we have to be considered in this group of letters and tracts
related to serious affairs, *An Account of Religion by Reason*.

III   *A Lady's Cold Sweat:* An Account of Religion by Reason

Aubrey's story of the writing of *An Account of Religion by
Reason* has been given above. Whatever the truth of its creation, *An
Account* is an undeniably curious and rather charming document.
Once again the reader is struck by the clarity and grace of
Suckling's prose and by the direct and orderly organization of his
ideas. *An Account* was directed to Edward Sackville, the fourth Earl
of Dorset, the father-in-law of Suckling's first cousin, Frances Cranfield, Lady Dorset. In the epistle to Dorset (September 2, 1637) accompanying the essay Suckling declares:

I send you here (my Lord) that Discourse enlarged, which frighted the
Lady into a cold sweat, and which had like to have made me an *Atheist* at
Court, and your Lordship no very good Christian. I am not ignorant that
the fear of *Socinianisme* at this time, renders every man that offers to give
an account of Religion by Reason, suspected to have none at all: yet I have
made no scruple to run that hazard, not knowing why a man should not use
the best weapon his Creator hath given him in his defence. . . . That man

is deceivable, is true; but what part within him is not likelyer to deceive him then his Reason? (169)

From this one might well expect a far more radical and rationalistic document than is actually found. What brought the lady to a sweat remains a mystery, at least for modern readers. The court discussion of the essay is supported by evidence of its circulation not long after it was written, and in his notes to *An Account* Mr. Clayton mentions that it was among the papers of a certain Mr. Vassall seized by government officials.

Perhaps modern difficulties with Suckling's *Account* are essentially responses to "Socinianism" itself. Very briefly Socinianism, which got its name from Fausto Paolo Sozzini (Latinized to Socinus), who advanced its major ideas in sixteenth-century Italy, was characterized primarily by its acceptance of the validity of the Scriptures and by its stress on the importance of reason in religion. Suckling's association with Socinianism, apart from the essay itself, is seen in the inclusion of John Hales, Lucius Cary, and William Chillingworth among the wits in "The Wits." All three were a part of the intellectual circle at Oxford which is associated with the foundation of the latitudinarian movement in the Church of England. "They were," one historian of religion has written, "true Broadchurchmen and apostles of tolerance."[4]

The passage already quoted from the epistle to the Earl of Dorset, is, it need hardly be argued, clearly and effectively expressed. If the style has not yet achieved the limpidity of, say, Dryden, or other prose stylists of the latter part of the century, it is clearly moving in that direction. Such a style suggests a matching clarity, openness, and logical neatness of thought. To a twentieth-century reader, however, the contents of the *Account* often seem at odds with the style; for the *Account* is in some measure quirky and eccentric. The quirkiness and eccentricity, nevertheless, belong more to the age than to Suckling in particular. Suckling's friend Sir William Davenant remembered being sent to the apothecary for powdered unicorn's horn when he was a young page and empirically testing the old tale that a spider could not get out of a circle made of powdered unicorn's horn (the spider could).[5] It helps to recall this early venture into experimental science when reading *An Account of Religion by Reason*.

The thesis of Suckling's essay is that belief in Christianity can be justified by reason. Although the argument takes some strange bends, the opening of the essay is relatively straightforward; the argument is that of uniform beliefs. Men in all times have believed in a deity. From the argument for a Superior Being Suckling moves to that of the Deity as Creator. If the argument for the existence of God because all men have believed in one suggests the unifor- mitarian rationalism of a later era, this argument for God as Creator surely suggests earlier philosophies: "For *if man made man, Why died not I when my Father died?* Since according to that great *Max- ime* of the Philosophers, *the cause taken away, the effect does not remain*" (170). This is a fairly typical example of the methods found in *An Account of Religion by Reason.* In a brief survey of beliefs shared by three ages, the Unknown, the Fabulous, and the Historical, which has been cited "as an early attempt at a com- parative study of religions,"[6] Suckling concludes that "a great part of our Religion, either directly or indirectly hath been professed by Heathens . . ." (172). Perhaps it is at this point that the lady men- tioned in the dedicatory epistle begins to break into her cold sweat.

That sweat might develop more with the assertion, "They con- cluded to be vices which we do; nor was there much difference in their vertues; onely Christians have made ready beleef the highest, which they would hardly allow to be any" (172). The apparent glance at the easy credulity of Christians and elevation of faith above reason is swift and almost unnoticeable, but the wry, skep- tical note is unmistakable. Nonetheless, Suckling does go on to argue for the superiority of Christian to pagan beliefs, centering his arguments on the absence of human and animal sacrifice, the Chris- tian view of the afterlife, and the nature of Christian ceremonies. As to the truth of Christianity in general he argues from the source, that is, the Apostles, finding them simple, true men. From general truths he turns to the specifics of Incarnation, Passion, Resurrection, and Trinity.

The details of these arguments don't need to be repeated here. The opening argument for the Incarnation is representative: ". . . That man should be made without man, why should we wonder more in that time of the world, then in the beginning? much easier, certainly, it was here, because neerer the natural way; Woman being a more prepared matter then earth" (176). Much the same is his view concerning the Resurrection: ". . . I conceive the difficulty to lie not so much upon our Lord, as us; it being with easie Reason imagined, that he which can make a body, can lay it down, and take it up again" (178). The juxtaposition of reason and imagination is paramount here. Reasonable for Suckling is what one can believe without too great a strain. In all of this there is a hint of "self-evident truths." ". . . *Nature, Substance, Essence, Hypostasis, Suppositum,* and *Persona,* have caused sharp disputes amongst the Doctors" (179), but clearly can be dismissed, and are, with an airy wave. "But in these high mysteries, similitudes (it may be) will be the best Arguments" (179). If the parenthesis is an apology (and it is hard to believe it really is), it is the only one in the *Account.* "Now, though I know this is so far from demonstration, that it is but imperfect instance (perfect being impossible of infinite by finite things) yet there is a resemblance great enough to let us see the possibility" (180). Quite far enough for a gentleman to go, at any rate, one must feel. And that, perhaps, is the outstanding quality of the *Account of Religion by Reason.* It is a gentleman's essay written for gentlemen. One really did not need to fuss quite so much with these questions once the obvious points have been made. There are pedants with ink-stained fingers for that sort of thing.

The modernity in the *Account* is in the feeling for the *consensus gentium* that will dominate the thinking of the age to come. The antirational skepticism of the essay also looks forward to positions of men like Dryden later in the century: ". . . it were stranger for me to conclude that God did not work *ad extra,* thus one and distinct within himself, because I cannot conceive how begotten, how proceeding; then if a Clown should say the hand of a Watch did not move, because he could not give an account of the wheels within. So far it is from being unreasonable, because I do not understand it, that it would be unreasonable I should . . ." (180). For all its oddities, then, the *Account* is a gentleman's essay and the witty turn at the end is distinctly that of Sir John Suckling, the court wit: "Thus much of Christian Profession compared with others: I should not shew which (compar'd within it self) ought to be preferred: but this is the work of every pen, perchance to the prejudice of Religion it self. This excuse (though) it has, that (like the chief Empire) having nothing to conquer, no other Religion to oppose or dispute against it, It hath been forced to admit of Civil wars, and suffer under its owne excellency" (180). One could no more justifiably complain that in straining for wit Suckling has violated truth here than one could make the same complaint of any poetic conceit.

An Account of Religion by Reason is certainly not exceptional or original theology or philosophy. The position Suckling takes is in its essentials that espoused by William Chillingworth in *The Religion*

of Protestants a Safeway of Salvation (1637) who believed, as Earl
Morse Wilbur has described, that "Only truths necessary to salvation need be sought for, and they are so plainly taught in Scripture,
and so few in number, that any open mind that will look for them
may see them."[7] The *Account* places Suckling within a clear current
of contemporary religious thought and with a group of loyal
Royalists who espoused a moderate religious position. At first glance
it might seem very surprising to find such an essay in the papers of
the rakehell gambler, courtier poet. But another look and one
recalls that Suckling was, after all, a Renaissance gentleman. His
ideal Hamlet was Ophelia's: "The courtier's, soldier's, scholar's,
eye, tongue, sword, / Th' expectancy and rose of the fair
state, / The glass of fashion and the mould of form . . ." (III, i,
150 - 52). The range of abilities and interests demonstrated by *An
Account of Religion by Reason* and by the letters is that of a
gentleman. It is no more surprising that Sir John wrote an essay on
religion than that he rode a horse, gambled, wenched, and wrote
letters on family affairs.

IV   *The Family Man: Advice and Sympathy*

It is unfortunate that only three of Suckling's letters directly
related to familial affairs have survived. The letters to Middlesex
might be considered family letters, but their subjects are not family
matters. The letter "To a Cosin (who still loved young Girles, and
when they came to be mariageable, quitted them, and fell in love
with fresh) at his fathers request, who desired he might be perswaded out of the humour, and marry" might be thought of as a family
letter, but it belongs to a distinct episotlary genre and can best be
considered elsewhere. The three letters are just enough to give a
tantalizing hint of this side of Suckling's character and to suggest
that he was a useful member of his family to whom one could turn
for help.

In one letter Suckling writes to his first cousin, Martha, Lady
Carey, reporting on the marriage negotiations for her daughter in
which he has been engaged. A letter of Lady Carey's to her father,
the Earl of Middlesex, has been preserved in which she asks her
father to "thanke Sir John for the care and paines he has taken in it
for me, in the treaty he put me in minde of" (199). Suckling's letter
has to do with a normal enough, prosaic family matter. It is clear
from it that the marriage negotiations have been complex and the

bargaining tight. What makes the letter striking is the consummate grace with which Suckling manages to move from business matters to romance, to clothe the whole with wit and style. The opening sentence must serve to illustrate the point: "It is none of the least discourtesies money hath done us Mortals, the making of things easie in themselves, and natural, difficult: Yong and handsome people would have come together without half this trouble, if it had never been . . ." (130). It is an elegant introduction to a business letter of this sort.

The other two family letters are one to his brother-in-law, Sir George Southcot, and the other to his sister Martha when Southcot ended their marriage by committing suicide. Both letters are marked with their own particular elegance. Martha Suckling married Sir George Southcot in July 1635; he was sixty years old and four times a widower. The chances for an unhappy marriage because of the disparity of ages were increased by Sir George's miserly nature. Suckling wrote Southcot on this subject on September 9, 1635, urging him to give up covetousness and reminding him that he had "entred into one of those neer conjunctions of which death is the onely honourable divorce . . ." (131).

The letter is graceful, elegant, and stylish but marked by an underlying mockery. The essence of the letter is the civil sneer. He reminds Southcot of his duty but cannot help jeering at the married man: "It faring with marryed men for the most part, as with those that at great charges wall in grounds and plant, who cheaper might have eaten Mellons elsewhere then in their owne Gardens Cucumbers" (131). Cold comfort for the miser to be told "that thing a husband is but Tenant for life in what he holds, and is bound to leave the place Tenantable to the next shall take it" (132). The fine barbs follow, one after the other; the expression is so polished we almost miss the venom: "The lure to which all stoop in this world, is either garnisht with pleasure or profit, and when you cannot throw her the one, you must be content to shew out the other" (132). If we met the passage out of context and unidentified, we should not hesitate to attribute it to some Jonsonian Truewit. A whole scene writes itself, the aging miserly gentleman, married to the lively extravagant lady, the urbane brother-in-law drawling his sardonic advice. But here, of course, it is life and not art. A gibe that must have particularly annoyed Sir George Southcot was Suckling's assertion that "Money in your hands is like the Conjurers Divel, which while you think you have that, has you" (133). At any rate,

Sir George found the remark worth mentioning in a letter of complaint to the Earl of Middlesex. At moments Suckling sounds like a divine, hitting delightfully sanctimonious notes: ". . . for while you have catcht at the shadow, uncertain riches, you have lost the substance, true content" (133). How infuriated Sir George must have been at such pieties from his rakehell brother-in-law. It is a shame that there are no more letters of advice to Southcot.

Fortunately the letter of "consolation" to Martha Lady Southcot after her husband's suicide in 1639 remains and is almost a masterpiece of its kind. At any rate, it is an exceedingly witty bit of irreverence. Suckling wastes no time on hypocritical pieties over Southcot's suicide:

It is so far from me to imagine this accident should surprize you, that in my opinion it should not make you wonder; it being not strange at all that a man who hath lived ill all his time in a house, should break a Window, or steal away in the night through an unusual Postern: you are now free, and what matter is it to a Prisoner whether the fetters be taken off the ordinary way or not. (149)

The similitudes reduce any possibility of actual sympathy, but the witty toughness itself so firmly establishes the context of wit that the irreverence passes as appropriate. Put more simply, the letter is more concerned with artful wittiness than with the actuality of the occasion. The occasion becomes the excuse for the demonstration of wit on a set theme.

"I would not have you so much enquire whether it were with his garters or his Cloak-bag strings" (149), the proverbial twang here, the comic baseness of garters and cloak-bag strings insure the continued toughness of tone and the blocking of emotion. An ensuing reference to "the Spanish Princesse *Leonina*" derived from the *New Epistles of Monsieur de Balzack* provides a further reminder of the literary nature of the letter. The outrageousness of the observation, "Of ill things the lesse we know, the better. Curiosity would here be as vain, as if a Cuckold should enquire whether it were upon the Couch or a Bed, and whether the Cavalier pull'd off his Spurrs first or not" (150) is tempered by the literary, crafted character of the letter. Necessarily to see character here, to ascribe the whole to an unfeeling, sneering rake is to miss the point of the wit of the seventeenth century.

Nevertheless, one can conclude pretty easily that neither Suckling nor his sister were much saddened by the suicide. Suckling does provide a pro forma admission that "I must confesse it is a just subject for our sorrow to hear of any that does quit his station without his leave that placed him there . . ." (150), but he goes on to cite Shakespeare and suicide as a "Roman's part" (*Julius Caesar*, V, iii, 89). (Witty, irreverent, and artful as the letter is, it is still difficult to avoid thinking of Southcot's suicide and this letter in relation to Suckling's own suicide just a few years later.) In tone and to a large degree in intent this letter could be placed with letters best classified as those of wit. It is the fact of the actuality of the occasion that makes it a "family" letter, but the wit, the freedom from cant, the implied sympathy, do, in fact, serve as appropriate consolation. The letter is above all that of an artist. Its consolation is deliberately irreverent; it aims at a sort of shocked laughter. In some sense it could have been written to an abstract, supposed addressee: "To a Lady Whose Miserly Husband Committed Suicide," but in this case, of course, the lady, the husband, and the suicide were real.

V   *Wit, Love, Manners, and Courtship*

Inevitably classification of these letters becomes somewhat muddled. Perhaps it would be more precise to make a distinction between uninhabited and inhabited letters, for many letters here could have been written by anyone to anyone; these are letters of pure wit, duty letters, even some of the love letters. Others of the letters grouped here are more clearly personal, but all are marked by the push toward wit and artifice. Furthermore, a number of the letters in this group belong to a distinct epistolary genre and are depersonalized by that fact.

Two early letters, both to William Wallis, one dated November 18, 1629, and the other May 5, 1630, illustrate the uninhabited letters. Each presents a series of witticisms. The effect is rather like that of a stand-up comedian delivering a series of one-liners. Neither letter has any particular pattern, neither really says anything either in terms of specific content or about the feelings of the writer. The subject of the first letter is the cross-Channel trip and the nature of the Dutch: "And sure their auncestors when they begott them thought on nothing but Munkeys, and Bores, and Asses, and such like ill favor'd creatures; for their Phisnomyes are soe wide from the rules of proportion, that I should spoyle my prose

to let in the description of them. In a word, they are almost as bad
as those of *Leicestershire*" (113). The level of craft is not very high,
and the joke is dull enough, but it is as carefully put together and as
unspontaneous as any music-hall or nightclub routine, even to the
turn at the end, "as bad as those of *Leicestershire*." We fleetingly
think, as we read the letter, that Suckling might have been carrying
a dog-eared joke book with him to idle away his shipboard hours.
What else can be said of such ancient wheezes? "The plague is here
constantly, I mean Excise; and in soe greate a manner, that the
whole Cuntry is sick on't. Our very Farts stand us in I know not how
much Excise to the States, before we let them" (113).

The other letter to Wallis represents no great advance in humor
and style, but at least develops an ingenious paradox that the inhabitants of the Netherlands have achieved a certain virtue because
of their poverty, "for being there is no money, there is no usury,
Nor no Corruption" (116, 117). In a passage quoted earlier Suckling
also finds the opportunity for mock praise of Catholicism: ". . . as
far as I conceive of it, it would suit well enough with us young men.
If a man be drunke overnight, it is but Confessing it next morning
or when he is sober, and the matter proves not Mortal. To the liing
with ones Sister, there is no more required than the telling the truth
of it to a ghostly father. And you may jumble as many wenches as
you please upon bedds, provided you wil but mumble as many
Avemaries upon beads" (117). The terminal pun is inevitable
enough; and these two letters to Wallis are perhaps most interesting
when set against the sober and businesslike accounts written at the
same time to the Earl of Middlesex, for they point to the various
personalities Suckling adopts in his letters. One must admit as well
that these two letters represent a lower order of wit and not Suckling at his best. Nor are the more clearly genre letters representative
of Suckling at his most polished. However, they are worth brief consideration as exemplars of the variety found in the letters and of
Suckling's use of available literary types.

Letter 48, addressed to some unknown *Ladies*, apparently
responds to a letter written either in a joking cryptograph or
perhaps just a very illegible hand. It gives us a brief glimpse of
fashionable joking, of the world of young court ladies giggling
behind their fans and composing a letter to the dashing and wicked
Sir John, who replies in part: "The Coronet believes there are noble
things in it; but what *Beaumont* said of worth wrapt up in rivelled
skin, he saith of this, Who would go in to fetch it out? . . . For

Mistresse T. there are in that, certaine *je ne scay quoys*, which none but those who have studied it can discover, and Sir *Anthony* shall hold his hand till Mr. *H.* comes to Town" (153). This suggests *L'Astrée*, maps of the court of love, and a whole range of precious foolery; at the same time, it is quite like the cryptic notes still to be found in high-school annuals suggesting romances in various states of repair.

"The Wine-drinkers to the Water-drinkers, greeting" gives us the Suckling not of the salon, but of the masculine world of the tavern, promising to send from the Bear "one of our Cabinet-Councel, Colonel *Young*, with some slight Forces of Canary, and some few of Sherry . . ." (154). It is directed to friends at Bath or some other watering place and is heavily facetious. The device of the letter is of formal diplomatic or military correspondence: "Whereas by Your Ambassador two dais since sent unto us, we understand that you have lately had a plot to surprize or (to speak more properly) to take the waters . . ." (153). The pun is typical of the whole. The "*Bear* at the *Bridge*-foot" was a tavern in Southwark at the end of London Bridge, popular with court wits. The letter is no more than a *jeu d'espirit*, but through it one can glimpse a bit of that tavern world inhabited by idle young gentlemen, wits, and poets. Inevitably the letter is clubbish and clannish.

That same quality is seen in the letter (No. 50) presumably to Thomas Carew with its little punning poem and rebus and a gloss following the verse: "In honest 'Prose thus: We would carry our selves first, and then our Friends, manage all the little Loves at Court, make more *Tower* work, and be the Duke of *B.* of our Age, which without it, we shall never be. Think on't therefore, and be assured, That if thou joyn'st me in the Patent with thee, in the height of all my greatness I will be thine, all but what belongs to *Desdemona*, which is just, as I mean to venture at thy Horse-race *Saturday* come seven-night" (155). The prose is not exactly "honest," rather it is that of the coterie and the private joke. But beyond this it is marked by a distinct exuberance. In these trivial letters to ladies, drinking companions, and cronies there is something of the bounce, verve, and bustle of a Mercutio.

The more clearly genre letters are almost as high spirited. "A Letter to a Friend to diswade him from marrying a Widow which he formerly had been in Love with, and quitted" (No. 51(a)) and the matching answer to it (No. 51 (b)), "A disswasion from Love" (No. 52), and "To a Cosin (who still loved young Girles, and when they came to be mariageable, quitted them, and fell in love with fresh) at his fathers request, who disired he might be perswaded out of the humour, and marry" (No. 53) belong to distinct epistolary types, examples of which can be found in Nicholas Breton's *Post with a Mad Packet of Letters.* In addition to the epistolary tradition the letters belong as well to the tradition of the paradox and the problem, such things as Donne's "That Women Ought to Paint" and "Why Hath the Common Opinion Afforded Women Soules?" immediately come to mind. These letters, then, are essays on set topics, the object being to explore the given topic in as ingenious, outrageous, and witty a fashion as possible.

The pair of letters on the pros and cons of marrying widows couples ingenuity with a mild sort of bawdry, presenting a kind of contest in *double entendre* and naturalistic cynicism: "After all this, to marry a *Widow,* a kind of *chew'd-meat!* What a fantastical stomach hast thou, that canst not eat of a dish til another man hath cut of it? Who would wash after another, when he might have fresh water for the asking?" (156). Against which is set the response to the problem in the answering letter: ". . . I'le marry a *Widow,* who is rather the *chewer,* then *thing chewed. . . . Wine* when *first broacht,* drinks not half so well as after a while *drawing.* Would you not think him a mad man who whilst he might fair and easily ride on the *beaten road-way,* should trouble himself with *breaking up* of *gaps?* . . . 'Tis *Prince*-like to marry a *Widow,* for 'tis to have a *Taster*" (157, 158). The witty similitudes are the point of the letters. Ingenuity is everything; the purported subject really doesn't matter. Instead, what counts is the play with the subject, the ingenious variations upon it. The manner is everything.

"A disswasion from Love" is directed to *Jack,* who may or may not be Jack Barry. The last paragraph mentions Mistress Howard and the Earl of Dorset, suggesting that the letter was more than just an epistolary exercise. But the preceding seven paragraphs are written in a standard genre again found in Nicholas Breton's *Post with a Mad Packet of Letters.* At any rate, the letter, with its advice on how to stay out or get out of love, is hardly serious advice. Once more the subject is of slight importance; the demonstration of wit is what counts. The usual advice to travel is rejected in favor of frequent visits to the loved one, in hopes of catching her at her worst. He is advised to see as many other beautiful girls as possible, moreover:

I would not have you deny your self the little things (for these Agues are
easier cured with Surfets than abstinence;) rather (if you can) tast all: for
that (as an old Author saith) will let you see
> That the thing for which we wooe,
> Is not worth so much ado.

(l58, 159)

The tired cynicism is part of the comic pose and is a note frequently
struck by Suckling.

The letter "To a Cosin (who still loved young Girles . . .) . . ."
belongs to the opposite genre type from the preceding, that is, a
persuasion to marriage rather than a dissuasion. However, Suckling
varies the pattern by adding a dry postscript: "I should have persuaded you to marriage, but to deal ingenuously, I am a little out of
arguments that way at this present: 'Tis honourable, there's no
question on't; but what more, in good faith I cannot readily tell"
(161). Suckling's cousin, Charles Suckling of Bracondale, may be
the "Honest Charles" addressed in the letter; he appears to have
married somewhat late and may have suffered from the Lolita syn-
drome attacked in the letter. "Honest Charles," however, is as likely to be a fictional addressee.

The comedy of the letter comes in large measure from the situation, but from the tone of cross, avuncular irritation as well: "Were
there not fooles enow before in the Common-Wealth of Lovers, but
that thou must bring up a new Sect? . . . Why the divel such yong
things? before these understand what thou wouldst have, others
would have granted. Thou dost not marry them neither, nor any
thing else. 'Sfoot it is the story of the Jack-an-apes and the Par-
tridges: thou starest after a beauty till it is lost to thee, and then
let'st out another, and starest after that till it is gone too . . ."
(160).

Throughout the whole runs a fashionable mix of libertine an-
tifeminism: "Women are like Melons: too green, or too ripe, are
worth nothing; you must try till you find the right one" (160). If
one is about ready to cry with Millamant, "truce with your
similitudes," one can still appreciate the ease of all this, its high
spirits and complete control of a particular manner. Something like
"voice" is difficult to locate and to describe in anything other than
impressionistic and subjective terms. But the letters, however one
puts it, do read very well aloud. There is a spoken quality to them in
the patterns of the sentences, in the timing of the jokes. Chunks of

them could be transferred to stage dialogue with little difficulty;
this spoken quality is certainly a part of Suckling's "ease."

The two groups of love letters are so marked by this quality of
ease coupled with craftsmanship—put another way, are so ar-
tificed—that a problem in dealing with them is in determining the
extent to which they represent real feelings and are indeed love
letters rather than exercises in the genre of the love letter. One
letter is to Anne Willoughby, and there is no doubt that Suckling's
attachment to her was financial rather than amatory. The letters fall
into two groups. The earlier group is directed to Suckling's first
cousin, Mary Cranfield; the later group to Mary Bulkeley, his
"Dear Princesse" and presumably his Aglaura. Suckling's actual
feelings for Mary Cranfield aren't known, and the letters really
don't reveal much. The florid declaration in the first letter, dated
October 30, 1629, "Let it suffice, that those countryes which I am
now to visit, are but soe many faire roomes in a prison, The whole
world it self, not yealding halfe that pleasure which your blest company can give!" (107) sets the tone for ensuing letters, and one is
more inclined to read it as mere compliment than heartfelt emotion.
The claim that his heart "hath been brought up under Platonicks,
and knows no other way of being paid for service, then by being
commanded more" (108) in the next letter is such palpable court
flummery that one is tempted to think of all of the letters in that
fashion. Yet in another letter (No. 3) there is enough sense of real
discourse that the debate remains open. The letter is apparently
written in response to a rebuke over gambling, something Suckling
"hitherto beleeved . . . to be . . . in it self as meerly indifferent as
Religion to a States-man . . ." and is acidic enough to be real:
"And now, since I know your Ladyship is too wise to suppose to
your self impossibilities, and therefore cannot think of such a thing,
as of making me absolutely good; it will not be without some im-
patience that I shall attend to know what sin you will be pleased to
assigne me in the room of this: something that has less danger about
it (I conceive it would be) and therefore if you please (Madam) let it
not be Women . . ." (109). There is not much of "Platonicks"
here.

Little enough of the actuality of the relationship, then, can be
drawn from the eight letters to Mary Cranfield, and after all what
really matters is paramountcy of style and manner above content
and feeling. A very short letter (No. 6) apologizing for not writing
demonstrates the skill with which Suckling is able to make the most

empty of social notes into an artistic event, and, out of nothing, invent an airy something. He has not written, he says, because he has nothing to say. This commonplace leads to the first witticism, a witticism set within the context of logical argument: "So, like Women that grow proud, because they are chaste; I thought I might be negligent, because I was not troublesom" (111). The finely balanced sentence has the effect of closure of a couplet in verse. If I could not rely on your goodness to forgive my neglect, I knew I could rely on your judgment, he goes on to argue. The compliment is effective precisely because it has the appearance of argument first and compliment second. Her judgment, he continues, will lead her to conclude that such trifles are of little worth and are not "necessary to the right honouring my Lady."

With this assertion he then moves to the concluding paragraph and the development of a witty paradoxical compliment that finishes the argument: "Your Ladyship I make no doubt, will take into consideration, that superstition hath ever been fuller of Ceremony then the true worship." The tightness of the prose, the careful design, the argumentative pattern, and the wit of it all bring the letter very close to verse. That is to say, its design, its compaction, its artifice belong to verse as much as to prose; all it lacks is rhyme and meter.

It is difficult to argue that the letters to Mary Bulkeley (if the letters assumed written to her actually were to her) are really much different from those to Mary Cranfield. If passion somehow equates with disorganization, these are not very passionate letters. In them one finds the same careful design, the crafting, and the feeling of distance that frequently comes with artifice. On the other hand, the affectionate epithet "Dear Princesse" and the assertions of the letters all point to a real feeling: "And oh! Why should I write then? Why should I not come my self? Those Tyrants, businesse, honour, and necessity, what have they to do with you and I? Why should we not do Loves commands before theirs whose Soveraignty is but usurped upon us? Shall we not smell to Roses 'cause others do look on? or gather them, 'cause there are prickles, and something that would hinder us?" (138). But finally to conclude much of Suckling's real feelings from passages such as this is a risky if not impossible task.

Letters to divers Eminent Personages reads in part the title page of the letters in the first edition of *Fragmenta Aurea*, and in *The Last Remains of Sir John Suckling* the title is *Letters to Several Per-*

sons of Honor. Both titles suggest the social and even public character of the letters. They may imply, or at least one should recognize, as well the sort of expectation Suckling's contemporaries would have in reading such letters. They would not be reading for biographical reasons and certainly not for psychological reasons. They would hardly expect personal revelations, nor, as should be clear, would they find any. Instead, they would read the letters, quite simply, for the style. They would look for—and find—in the letters the same elegance, wit, and control they found in the poetry. Generally speaking, those letters in which something of a personal voice can be detected, for the most part those letters relating to serious military and political affairs, were not published in either *Fragmenta Aurea* or *The Last Remains*. The letters published in those works were those displaying their author at his public best. One doesn't look at Van Dyck portraits for revelation of character, but for brilliant portrayal of surfaces and for the creation of a particular world through his art. So too with Suckling's prose.

CHAPTER 3

The Plays: The Sad One
and Aglaura

I *Cavalier Drama*

S UCKLING has left us three completed plays, *Aglaura, The Goblins, Brennoralt, or The Discontented Colonel,* and an unfinished work, *The Sad One.* In addition there remains "A Prologue of the Author's to a Masque at Wiston" in *The Last Remains.* The masque itself is lost, but it may have been written by Suckling. Even though one can agree with their modern editor, L. A. Beaurline, that "none of them is a good play by our standards,"[1] the plays are interesting both for themselves and for the light they throw on Suckling and his times. He was, after all, writing for a seventeenth-century audience and not for us. *Aglaura* was famous, even popular in its day, and all three plays survived their author to be revived in the Restoration. The plays are firmly locked into the world of the court of Charles I. Although there is clear evidence of production at court of only *Aglaura,* Suckling himself is, with certain qualifications, a courtier playwright, and his work needs to be seen within the context of court drama. A major qualification, as always with Suckling, is that he is willing to mock the very mode in which he writes.

If one examines a list of the plays of the Caroline period, from 1626 until the closing of the theaters in 1642, one can find some very fine plays, most of them comedies. Ben Jonson's great period was over, but from the works of Sir William Davenant, James Shirley, Richard Brome, Philip Massinger, and the one tragic writer who still retains some currency, John Ford, one can without strain claim at least a dozen or more plays capable of holding a contemporary audience with more than antiquarian interest. These were

57

professional playwrights who knew their trade and could appeal to dramatic universals apart from restricted local and temporal interests.

The merits of the courtier playwrights, with whom Suckling must be numbered, are less easily discerned. The problem, however, often rests more with the nature of the court play than with the playwright. After noting the degree of spectacle and the number of songs in William Cartwright's *The Royal Slave*, produced both at Oxford and at court just a year before *Aglaura*, G. Blakemore Evans goes on to locate the salient features of court drama: "The point to be observed is that it took more than mere spectacle and sound to please the court; something was still demanded from the play. What this something was may be summed up as follows: an exotic usually serious plot dealing with exalted and unreal characters, moving in an atmosphere falsely moral and saturated with doctrines of a sentimentalized and sophisticated Neoplatonism, the whole tricked out in a many-colored rhetorical coat."[2] Such a description is hardly an encouraging invitation to court drama, but unfortunately only too true.

The extraordinarily strong interest of Charles I's court in the stage and its influence on the courtier playwrights is most easily exemplified by recalling that Queen Henrietta Maria not only liked seeing plays but also enjoyed taking part in theatrical productions herself. The most famous instance of this regal involvement occurred on January 9, 1633, when the queen took the role of Queen Bellesa in Walter Montague's more than tedious pastoral, *The Shepherd's Paradise*. Suckling memorializes Montague's play in "The Wits":

> *Wat Montague* now stood forth to his tryal,
> And did not so much as suspect a denial;
> Wise *Apollo* then asked him first of all
> If he understood his own Pastoral
>   For
> If he could do it, 'twould plainly appear
> He understood more than any man there,
> And did merit the Bayes above all the rest,
> But the Mounsieur was modest, and silence confest.
>   (74 - 75, 81 - 88)

The gibe at Montague reflects the florid wordiness of the pastoral, but above all its arcane preciousness. Montague had been involved in the marriage negotiations of the king and queen and served as an attaché in the English embassy in Paris, and had later converted to Catholicism. There was plenty of reason to call him "Mounsieur," but the epithet was earned as well by the thoroughly French nature of *The Shepherd's Paradise.*

Undoubtedly all 175 closely printed pages of love debate, discussion of ethical problems, trials and tribulations of lovers, summaries of romances and endless talk should be left to its deserved oblivion save that it provides so extreme an example of courtly taste. The queen and her ladies must have read rather than memorized their parts,[3] but even a reading production taxes the imagination. How could one bear to speak and hear such lines?

BASILINO: I must no longer, Fidamira, trust my infant virtue against the growing strength of thy beauty which improves in this thy interdiction of them. I'le leave you, Fidamira, and without asking any thing, not so much as, Who is that Subject, so much richer than his Prince by the consignment of your faith; And I doubt not but the heavens think me so fully punished as they will ne'r consent to the breach of this my vow, of ever being guilty even of the directist solicitation of your love. And some auspicious deity antedates this ease unto me, the belief that no other man shall ever injoy the matchlesse *Fidamira.*[4]

Bellesa, much later on, is furious when Moramente kisses her hand when she is asleep. She is even more furious when the repentent gentleman asks that he be punished:

BELLESA: Tis a new insolence, this punishment you aske, that I should descend so low as but think upon your body. [I] shall think your minde lesse worthy than I did, and so much, I shall not think it very sensible of its declination in my thoughts.[5]

Such delicate sensibilities define the nature of *préciosité* and illustrate as well the cult of court Platonism which Henrietta Maria brought with her from France. The world of Honoré D'Urfé's *L'Astrée* is moved to the stage, and the elegancies of the Hôtel de Rambouillet are transferred to the English court.[6] Suckling scoffs at all this precious Neoplatonism as so much unintelligible stuff, and Alfred Harbage is surely correct in saying "most Englishmen, even at court, were apt to be unimpressed by involved pretense—especially by the unpointed ardors of platonic courtship, which seemed to them a species of grouse-shooting without the grouse";[7] nonetheless, *The Shepherd's Paradise*, bad as it is, represents the sort of thing the court enjoyed and a style within which, and at other times against which, Suckling wrote.

II   *A Trial Run:* The Sad One

The Sad One is incomplete, but its plot provided some of the material for *Aglaura;* and a number of lines are reworked in the latter play. We need not take very seriously the ingenuous remarks of the publisher Humphrey Moseley in "To the Reader" of *The Last Remains of Sir John Suckling* (1659), where the play first appeared: "I hope I shall not need to crave your pardon for publishing this Dramatick Piece of Sir *John Suckling*, (Imperfect I cannot say, but rather unfinish'd) there being a kind of Perfection even in the most deficient Fragments of this incomparable Author."[8] "Imperfect," in fact, is a perfectly good description of *The Sad One*. It is hard not to feel its imperfections were the cause of its incompletion, that Suckling gave up on it because he felt he could not rescue it. If in nothing else, Suckling was at least thrifty artistically, and *The Sad One* became both a trial run and a sort of literary spare parts room for *Aglaura*.

Many verbal parallels with *Aglaura*, however, seem more likely to be memorial echoes than deliberate reworkings.

> When Fortunes hang in doubt,
> Bravely to dare, is bravely to get out.
>   (I, ii, 35 - 36)

is in *Aglaura:*

> When Fortunes, honour, life, and all's in doubt,
> Bravely to dare, is bravely to get out.
>   (III, i, 6 - 7)

Other memories or echoes are less exact. In *The Sad One* one finds:

> For souls, at such a time, like ships in tempests
> Throw out all they have.
>   (IV, iv, 68 - 69)

This is rephrased in *Aglaura:*

> And like dull sea-men threatened with a storme
> Throw all I have away, to save my selfe.
>
> (III, ii, 130 - 31)

We can debate endlessly and fruitlessly to what extent these and other parallels (Beaurline cites fourteen in his commentary) are strictly considered reworkings or simply echoes from memory or a casual rereading of the manuscript, but a close relationship to *Aglaura* is clear.

The Sad One was written sometime before 1637 when *Aglaura* appeared. The disgraced and mistreated courtier, Old Clarimont, and allusions to the Duke of Buckingham point to Suckling's concern over the disgrace of his uncle, the Earl of Middlesex, and Buckingham's connection with it; these concerns are most evident in Suckling's letters between 1629 and 1631. Beaurline's conclusion that *The Sad One* may have been written sometime after Suckling's return from the continent in the spring of 1632 is convincing.

The Sad One is, as has been said, an incomplete practice play, a trial run, and as such of little intrinsic merit. The materials of the play are the commonplaces of Caroline theater—the Sicilian setting (or rather the setting in a romantic never-never land called Sicily), the intrigue ridden court, a good old courtier murdered in prison, his son's vow of revenge, the lecherous king, the immoral but repentant lady, the brother as bawd, the cuckolded husband, attempted regicide, and an abundance of talk and high sentiments. In sum, it has all the ingredients—blood, sex, and rant, but they are not pullled together.

The characterization is very slight. There is a fairly lively parody of Ben Jonson in the figure of the poet Multecarni (a nice name for a fat man), busy producing an obviously execrable masque, but apart from him the characters are unmemorable.

Old Clarimont, unjustly imprisoned, opens the play with sententious reflections:

> The clap o'th' Vulgar, and loud popular applause,
> Are not the Eccho of our Acts, but Fortunes.
> Great men but Dials are, which when the Sun
> Is gone, or hides his face, are hardly lookt upon.
>
> (I, i, 22 - 25)

Fortunately he is quickly murdered by the wicked Lorenzo, who is also the vehicle for some sneers in Marlovian style at the late favorite of King James, the Duke of Buckingham:

> And all the while thou, like my *Ganimede*,
> Shalt taste *Ambrosia* with me, while the petty gods
> Burst with repining at they happiness:
> Thou shalt dispose of all, create, displace,
> Be call'd my Boy, revel and mask, what not?
>
> (III, ii, 29 - 33)

Lorenzo meets a richly deserved fate when he is tricked into killing his father and then is himself killed. It is, as King Aldebrand says, ". . . most sad and strange!" (III, iv, 13). Even stranger is the fact that the king chooses this bloody moment to tell young Clarimont that he is in love with Clarimont's sister, Francelia, the wife of Florelio. Clarimont's predicament is one dear to the hearts of many dramatists of the period, one found again in *Aglaura:*

> Was there no woman in the Court
> To feed thy lust with, but my sister,
> And none to be the Bawd but I?
>
> (III, iv, 57 - 59)

There is, then, no lack of sensational dramatic material, but if that is a redeeming feature, it is one of the few in the play. The primary dramatic problem is that there is no adequate complication between the reason for revenge and the taking of revenge. If Suckling had finished the play, Francelia's lover, the Favorite, Bellamine, and most likely the king as well would have been killed in spectacular and noisy scenes. But the problem of providing interesting situations before those final scenes was not solved.

Obviously the matter is at some distance from the tedious decorousness of *The Shepherd's Paradise*. If one accepts the view that Cavalier plays "are decorous, indeed very solemn things,"[9] one would have to put *The Sad One* outside that tradition. Its sensationalism belongs earlier to Fletcher, more immediately to Ford. It partakes both of the courtly, Cavalier fashions and those of the popular stage. Its conventionality is not restricted; it happily absorbs all the theatrical conventions of the period. The sensationalism, the unnatural and undefined characters, the high rhetoric, all belong to the age. What one sees, then, in *The Sad One* is Suckling trying his hand at those conventions, working with plot and dialogue, acknowledging the expansion of the poet-courtier role—surely with one eye on the main chance and the professional theater.

The play is unfinished and clearly something from the workshop, but it has its moments. The hits at Ben Jonson are spirited enough—he is all confidence and critical disdain, "If it does not take, my masters, it lies not upon me, I have provided well; and if the stomack of the times be naught, the fault's not in the meat or in the Cook. Come, let's find out *Lepido* and dine at the Mermaid—" (IV, v, 24 - 27). Multecarni's masque, had it been written, would have provided one of the major scenes in the play and a greatly expanded parody of Jonson. The brilliant song "Hast thou seen the Doun ith' air" in IV, iv is a thoroughly successful take-off on Jonson's lyric "Have you seen but a bright lily grow" in *The Devil is an Ass*. Indeed, the song provides the play with its one moment of sheer brilliance, but the dramatic setting is awkwardly done.

Probably the best that can be said for *The Sad One* is that it shows Suckling thoroughly conversant and willing to experiment with the dramatic conventions of the day. In large measure this is to say that he recognized the requirements of spectacle, sensation, high-flown and witty language, the *précieuse* interest in static debate over Platonic quiddities, and above all, a sustained and unremitting unreality. All of these qualities, however, can best be examined in Suckling's next and most famous dramatic endeavor, *Aglaura*.

III   Aglaura: *"An Unheard of Prodigality"*

When Suckling turned to the stage, he did so with characteristic extravagance. *Aglaura* was elaborately and most expensively produced. According to John Aubrey the poet footed the bill himself, and the costumes were "very rich; no tinsell, all the lace pure gold and silver. . . ."[10] This spectacle was produced in late January or early February of 1638 by the King's Company at Blackfriars and before the king and queen at court. Next, with a new fifth act, the play, converted from tragedy to tragicomedy, was given another production before the king and queen at the Cockpit Theater on April 3.

Not content simply with the expensive and flashy productions, Suckling printed *Aglaura* in folio, another ostentation which

produced various amused and critical comments, including the
poem by Richard Brome mentioned earlier. The folio with its wide
margins and unused spaces was probably printed by Suckling at his
own cost as a souvenir to present to the members of the audience at
the court performance.[11] It is also probable that the extant
manuscript of the play, formerly in the Royal Library, was made as
a presentation copy for the king.

All this puffery is typical enough of Sir John; the gesture is that of
his hundred horse. The play, then, must be seen to a great extent as
another courtly flourish, one more dazzling demonstration of Sir
John Suckling's versatility. There is very little in it, save the songs,
that can appeal to our age; a revival of *Aglaura* now is unthinkable.
But it held the stage in its own day and beyond, even being revived
with apparent success after the Restoration. As late as 1691 Gerard
Langbaine could still write of it, "This play is much priz'd at this
day."[12] Samuel Pepys read it on September 5, 1664, and found it "a
mean play; nothing of design in it."[13] On January 10, 1668, he went
". . . to the King's house, to see 'Aglaura,' which hath been always
mightily cried up, and so I went with mighty expectation, but do
find nothing extraordinary in it all, and but hardly good in any
degree." Judgments regarding its quality may have varied, but its
reputation, at any rate, was bright for longer than one might think.

Perhaps the most disturbing critical problem concerning *Aglaura*
is that is has two interchangeable last acts, a tragic version and a
happy-ending tragicomic version. This is the funeral baked meats
furnishing the marriage tables with a vengeance. How is one to deal
with a dramatic creation that takes itself with so little seriousness, a
play in which the events of the first four acts have so little inevitability of conclusion that the playwright can, without a qualm of
conscience, reverse the play's ending?

> Tis strange perchance (you'll thinke) that she that di'de
> At Christmas, should at Easter be a Bride:
> But 'tis a privilege the Poets have,
> To take the long-since dead out of the grave.
>
> (96, 1 - 4)

Suckling's comments in the "Prologue to the Court" of the
tragicomic version are lighthearted; the obvious conclusion must be
that we aren't meant to consider the matter seriously. Integrity of

design, thematic inevitability, dramatically logical consequences, artistic "truth," then, are not of concern to Suckling in *Aglaura*. The critical standards one applies to "serious" works aren't applicable to the play. It is an entertainment, far more elaborate than juggling or tightrope walking, but in the sense of making a coherent statement about life or striving toward something we might call "art" it is finally entertainment in exalted garb. Its spectacle suggests the masque and its later development, opera. It combines the spectacle and elegance of grand opera with the intellectual vacuity of most musical comedies. Its strengths are those of an entertainment, and it should be judged as such.

IV   *The Plot: "Here's a How-de-do"*

Aglaura takes place in a world of varied and astounding calamities which recalls at once W. S. Gilbert and the soap operas of television. It is a world whose *dramatis personae* achieve their identities through their relationships in love and in lust: the King, "Lustfull and cruel, in love with *Aglaura*"; Thersames, "Prince, in love with *Aglaura*"; Orbella, "Queene, at first Mistresse to *Ziriff:* in love with *Ariaspes*"; Ariaspes, "Ambitious, Brother to the King"; Ziriff, "Otherwayes ZORANNES disguised, Captaine of the Guard, in love with *Orbella*, brother to *Aglaura*, a blunt brave." The essence of the plot should be clear just from these excerpts from the list of characters. The play is compounded of confusions of love, the lust of the monarch, disguise, intrigue, and, of course, an abundance of talk with the addition of Orsames, "A young Lord antiplatonique," and Semanthe, "In love with *Ziriff*, platonique."

The play opens with a device Suckling must have learned from his reading of Shakespeare, that of introducing the characters to the stage in the middle of a conversation:

JOLAS: Married? and in *Diana's* Grove!
JOLINA: So was th'appointment, or my Sense deceiv'd me.
JOLAS: Married!
      Now by those Powers that tye those prettie knots,
      'Tis verie fine, good faith 'tis wondrous fine.

                                     (I, i, 1 - 5)

John Dryden, so Beaurline reminds us,[14] admired these lines sufficiently to echo them in *The Wild Gallant* (V, v, 60 - 63):

Married!
And in Diana's Grove boy.
Why 'tis fine by heaven; 'tis wondrous fine; as the Poet goes on sweetly.

The marriage is that of Prince Thersames and Aglaura, a rash act
that, given the King's inordinate lust for the lady, can only lead to
disaster. When, at last, the newlyweds are together and Thersames
is panting with proper, or perhaps improper, ardor:

> . . . come! undoe, undoe,
> And from these envious clouds slide quicke
> Into Loves proper Sphere, thy bed.
>
> (I, vi, 25 - 27)

there comes the fatal knock on the door; Zorannes / Ziriff arrives
with the horrid news "The King must have her _____" (I, vi,
43). Earlier, however, Zorannes / Ziriff has identified himself in
soliloquy as a lover and revenger:

> Three tedious Winters have I waited here,
> Like patient Chymists blowing still the coales,
> And still expecting, when the blessed houre
> Would come, should make me master of
> The Court *Elixar*, Power, for that turnes all:
> 'Tis in projection now; downe, sorrow, downe,
> And swell my heart no more, and thou wrong'd ghost
> Of my dead father, to thy bed agen,
> And sleepe securely—
> It cannot now be long, for sure *Fate* must,
> As't has been cruell, so, a while be just.
>
> (I, ii, 21 - 31)

However, the not very Hamletlike Zorannes is certainly, as Fredson
Bowers asserts, "a cardboard revenger,"[15] and the theme of his
revenge is subordinated by concern with the love story of Thersames and Aglaura. Still another complication is added by the fact
that the Queen and Ariaspes, the brother of the King, are plotting
the death of the King so that Ariaspes may replace him on the
throne and in the bed. The consequences of all this intrigue are
bloody in the extreme:

> What have wee here? a Church-yard? nothing
> But silence, and grave?
>
> (V (t), iii, 163 - 64)

Orsames asks when he views the final carnage.

The King is killed by his own men who have set a trap for Thersames, a plot foiled and counterplotted by Zorannes, who then kills his rival Ariaspes in a fair duel after surprising him. Thersames is killed by Aglaura, who mistakes him for the King; she dies immediately upon recognizing her error. Zorannes is poisoned by the Queen and that lady is, in turn, stabbed by Pasithas, Zorannes's "faithful servant, blunt." A variety of minor figures also meet their dooms in concert with their betters. All this bloodshed, of course, is averted in the tragicomic version of the fifth act. Aglaura still stabs Thersames by mistake, but so inefficiently that he is able to remark with considerable wit under the circumstances:

> Loves wounds us'd to be gentler than these were;
> The paines they give us have some pleasure
> In them, and that these have not.
> (V (c), i, 116 - 18)

The King and Queen both repent, the former vowing three years' penitence, the latter submitting appreciatively to an indefinite term in "Diana's Nunnerie." The unrepentant Ariaspes is allowed to depart, cursing and gnashing his teeth, for eternal banishment.

Suckling's source for the plot of *Aglaura* was most likely the account of the love of Prince Darius and Aspasia in Plutarch's *Life of Artaxerxes*. L. A. Beaurline notes the existence of two dramatic versions of the same story in French: Jean Desmarets de Saint Sorlin's *Aspasie* (1636) and *Le Couronnement de Darie* (1642) by François le Metel de Boisrobert.[16] He suggests the possibility that Suckling's play may have influenced Boisrobert or that they may have shared a common source in the Italian tragicomedy *Dario Coronato* (1611). Whatever its origins, in summation the plot is likely to strike the modern reader as, at the least, extravagant, but the point is that the plot was eminently appropriate for the entertainment Suckling wanted to create.

V *A Fashionable Bouquet*

The plot of *Aglaura* more than adequately provided varied and lively stage action. The action can't be taken very seriously and it is clear that Suckling did not take it so himself. Pepys's complaint that he found "nothing of design in it" is really beside the point, as are objections to a patent insincerity, lack of internal logic, and absence of real characterization. The play needs to be approached on its own terms, which will explain its popularity in the seventeenth century and identify its particular merits.

The interpretation suggested by L. A. Beaurline is most useful.[17] No single description of the play really works. *Aglaura* is not a failed revenge play, a Platonic drama, an anti-Platonic libertine drama, or even a "Fletcherian tragedy of court intrigue, with greater excesses and complications and a more fetid and unwholesome atmosphere."[18] Instead, it contains elements of all of these types, but no single pattern will fit it completely. The often-quoted observation of Richard Flecknoe in his *Short Discourse of the English Stage* is apropos: ". . . as *Beaumont* and *Fletcher* first writ in the Heroick way, upon whom *Suckling* and others endeavoured to refine agen; one saying wittily of his *Aglaura* that 'twas full of fine flowers, but that they seem'd rather stuck then growing there. . . ."[19]

"If all the disparate elements form a semblance of a whole," Beaurline argues, "they are unified only in the theme"; he finds the theme to be that "the consummation of love in virtuous marriage is the suitable end of the love game."[20] If there is a theme, that surely is it. But both the "ifs" of unity and theme are large ones. A more fruitful approach is not to look for unity and for a single developed theme, but rather to examine those "fine flowers . . . rather stuck then growing there."

Suckling's own view of dramatic design expressed in the Epilogue to the tragicomic version:

> Plays are like Feasts, and everie Act should bee
> Another Course, and still varietie.
>
> (114, 1 - 2)

hardly argues for unity and consistency. Instead it points to exactly what one finds in *Aglaura*, a search for novelty, variety, and crowd-pleasing moments. Given the nature of Suckling's crowd, fashion is central to it all.

The elaborate and expensive costuming has already been mentioned. To this feature must be added the use of painted scenes which, as John Aubrey says not quite correctly, "in those days were only used at Masques."[21] Beaurline believes that an unidentified sketch of a forest scene among Inigo Jones's drawings is actually a drawing of a scene for *Aglaura*.[22] William Cartwright's *Royal Slave* also had scenery, that is, painted scenes on flats which formed a changeable background for the action. Such scenes were not, as Aubrey says, limited to masques, but they were derived from masques and were exceedingly rare on public stages. Suckling's use of painted scenes in the theater at Blackfriars has its place in stage history, and his friend William Davenant would firmly transfer the use of painted scenes to the public theater in the Restoration.

The real point here, however, is that Suckling saw his play as a spectacle, richly costumed and fitted out with the painted scenes of that quintessentially aristocratic entertainment, the masque. Everything in the play points to fashion, and it is fashion that determines the contents of the play.

Dryden praised Beaumont and Fletcher because ". . . they understood and imitated the conversation of gentlemen . . .; whose wild debaucheries, and quickness of wit in repartees, no poet can ever paint as they have done."[23] In the same essay Dryden notes Suckling's special regard for Shakespeare, but despite that regard, it is obvious that Suckling followed the lead of Beaumont and Fletcher in imitating the "conversation of gentlemen." "The power of conversing well is always the noblest and most reliable equipment of gentlemen," Kathleen Lynch astutely remarks, "no matter what pressing demands for heroic action in mazes of exotic adventure Suckling's luxuriant imagination may foist upon them."[24]

Central to the fashionable quality of *Aglaura* is its conversation, its language—witty, graceful, and copious. Its wit is that of the similitude, and if, as Dr. Johnson says, the quibble was Shakespeare's fatal Cleopatra, so was the similitude for Suckling. "Confidence!" cries Zorannes,

> (Thou paint of women, and the States-mans wisdome,
> Valour for Cowards, and of the guilties Innocence,)
> Assist mee now.—
>
> (IV, i, 23 - 26)

The parenthesis is hardly parenthetical; the similitude is more important than the plea itself.

Ariaspes is an out-and-out villain and Queen Orbella no better than she should be, but they court and plan murder with highflown, poetic language, Ariaspes touching on Neoplatonic theory and Orbella finely reflecting on mutability:

> ARIASPES. By this—and this—loves break-fast: *Kisses her*
> By his feasts too yet to come,
> By all the beautie in this face,
> Divinitie too great to be prophan'd—
> ORBELLA. O doe not sweare by that;
> Cankers may eat that flow'r upon the stalke,
> (For sicknesse and mischance, are great devourers)
> And when there is not in these cheeks and lips,
> Left red enough to blush at perjurie,
> When you shall make it, what shall I doe then?
> ARIASPES. Our soules by that time (Madam)
> Will by long custome so acquainted be,
> They will not need that duller truch-man Flesh,
> But freely, and without those poorer helps,
> Converse and mingle; meane time wee'll teach
> Our loves to speake, not thus to live by signes,
> And action is his native language, Madam,
>   *Enter* ZORANNES *unseene.*
> This box but open'd to the sense will doe't.
>   (II, iii, 58 - 75)

The box, of course, is poison. It would be absurd to think that villains cannot chatter as fashionably as heroes; nor is it meant to suggest that some sort of villainous diction is demanded. Rather, the effect of the chatter is to deflect consideration of Ariaspes and Orbella in their villainous character. Instead one notices their verbal skills, their conversational grace. A murder is planned, but the language bears no relation to it. It is fine talk, elegant, fashionable, but oddly suited to the scene.

Zorannes is a hidden observer and listener. His response might have been dramatic—at least a burst of high stage bombast. Instead it is reflective and refined:

> ZORANNES. Then all my feares are true, and shee is false:
> False as a falling Star, or Glow-wormes fire:
> This Devill Beautie is compounded strangely,
> It is a subtill point, and hard to know,
> Whether't has in't more active tempting,
> Or more passive tempted; so soon it forces,
> And so soone it yeelds—
>   (II, iii, 82 - 88)

It is not simply the modish antithesis of "true" and "false" of the opening lines that establishes its gentility, but the reflective elaboration of thought as well. The questions of the nature of beauty, the active and passive, are worthy of Donne, and indeed, the couplet with which Zorannes concludes his resolution to seek revenge:

> To love is noble frailtie, but poore sin
> When we fall once to Love, unlov'd agen.
> (II, iii, 99 - 100)

even may suggest lines from Donne's "Love's Deitie," a poem Suckling parodied in "O! for Some honest lover's ghost":

> Correspondencie
> Only his subject was; It cannot be
> Love, till I love her, that loves mee.[25]

Even more striking examples of Suckling's concern for the fashionable moment can be seen in the recurring references to the popular doctrines of court Platonism. In I, v, for example, a transition scene to allow Thersames and Aglaura time to reach their frustrating bedroom, the action of the play is completely arrested while Semanthe, Orithie, Orsames, and Philan ring the changes on the theme of fruition. Orithie responds indignantly to Orsames's assertion that dogs and lovers "both alike must be / Flesh't in the chase" (I, v, 14 - 15):

ORITHIE. Will you then place the happiness, but there,
         Where the dull plow-man and the plow-mans horse
         Can finde it out? Shall soules refin'd, not know
         How to preserve alive a noble flame,
         But let it die, burne out to appetite?
                                     (I, v, 16 - 20)

As so often in the plays, Suckling here echoes his own verse. The same comic argument is made in "Against Fruition" ("Stay here fond youth and ask no more, be wise"):

> Urge not 'tis necessary, alas! we know
> The homeliest thing which mankind does is so;
> The World is of a vast extent we see,
> And must be peopled; Children then must be;
> So must bread too; but since there are enough
> Born to the drudgery, what need we plough?
> (37, 13 - 18)

These ultraaristocratic pretensions of the precious Court Platonists
are ridiculed in Sir William Davenant's comic assault on *préciosité*,
The Platonic Lovers (1636), in identical terms:

> PHYLOMONT. But who shall make men, sir; shall the world cease?
> THEANDER. I know not how th'are made, but if such deeds
> Be requisite, to fill up armies, villages,
> And city shops; that killing, labour, and
> That coz'ning still may last, know, Phylomont,
> I'd rather nature should expect such coarse
> And homely drudgeries from others than
> From me.[26]

Suckling, then, works in *Aglaura* a current sophisticated joke for all
it is worth.

The scene is entirely static in terms of action and of plot development. Its only movement is that of witty conversation and its only
development conversational. The fruition theme is expanded upon
as Orsames and Philan cleverly describe Love's dining habits:

> PHILAN.   Sometimes a cheeke plumpt up
>   With broth, with creame and clarret mingled
>   For sauce, and round about the dish
>   Pomegranate kernells, strew'd on leaves of Lillies.
> ORSAMES. Then will he have black eies, for those of late
>   He feeds on much, and for varietie
>   The gray—
> PHILAN.   You forget his cover'd dishes
>   Of *Je-ne-scays-quas* and Marmalade of lips,
>   Perfum'd by breath sweet as the beanes first blossomes.
>   (I, v, 29 - 37)

The effect worked for, apart from the prettiness of the conceit, is of
the impromptu ingenuity of two courtier wits. What is said matters
less than how it is said; (and how finely it is said!) if the scene is like
one of those stuck flowers about which Flecknoe complained, it is so
intentionally. The scene exists first of all for its demonstration of
style, for the display of gentlemen talking *comme il faut*.

VI *Spectacle and Scene: "If Pleasures be Themselves but Dreames"*

The language of *Aglaura* is often essentially detached from the
action. Conversations, figures, jokes will exist for themselves. The

audience listens for elegancies of wit, not for revelation of characters or for language tied to them in image and tone. The individual flowers are to be admired. The same sort of effect is found in the action of the play. Scenes can exist for their conversation, that is, for conversational set pieces or tours de force, or for a particular sort of theatrical effect. The sexual frustrations of Thersames are dramatized not for matters of character or plot, but for subject and sensation.

One way of looking at *Aglaura* is to see it as a kind of review, a dramatic potpourri, intentionally so designed, in which individual scenes are more important than the design of the whole. The second scene of act four, which contains one of Suckling's finest songs, "Why so pale and wan fond Lover," is one such scene. L. A. Beaurline has discussed the poem in its dramatic context;[27] here, the scene can be looked at as a kind of review "turn." The action is not advanced by the scene; nothing really happens. Nor does one learn more about any of the characters in it. The fifty-five lines of the scene are in large measure—except as providing for the passing of time and a transition—dramatically useless. A song is sung, framed in witty chit-chat and heard in a particular fashion:

> ORITHIE. Is the Queene ready to come out?
> PHILAN. Not yet sure, the King's brother is but newly entred.
> SEMANTHE. Come, my Lord, the Song then.
> ORITHIE. I! The Song.
>
> (IV, ii, 1 - 4)

The song, it can be argued, is demanded by the courtiers because a song was frequently used in plays to denote sexual intercourse occurring off-stage.[28] So the scene opens with a covert allusion to the Queen's adulterous relationship with her brother-in-law. The song, with its anti-Platonic theme, gains a certain piquancy because of the implied sexual situation. The Queen and Ariaspes may be, at that very moment, following the libertine injunctions the song suggests. Orbella's own entrance and her subsequent wry and anti-Platonic comments on the antics of lovers are also interestingly touched by the subterranean sexuality of the scene:

> ORBELLA. These Lovers sure are like Astronomers,
>   That when the vulgar eye discovers, but
>   A Skie above, studded with some few Stars,
>   Finde out besides strange fishes, birds, and beasts.
>
> (IV, ii, 44 - 47)

This short scene, then, exists for the song, but the song is so framed that it colors the scene, making it suggestively risqué, almost voyeuristic. Thus it becomes a kind of independent dramatic "turn," albeit one marked by considerable sophistication.

The other song in *Aglaura*, "No, no, faire Heretique . . . ," is less interestingly framed, but serves to elaborate one of the thematic concerns of the play, the proper balancing of emotions in love:

> For Love growne cold or hot,
> Is Lust, or Friendship, not
>   The thing wee have;
> For that's a flame would die,
> Held downe, or up to high:
>   (IV, iv, 17 - 21)

This is, the audience is told by the boy who sings it to the sad Aglaura, Thersames's song. The balance it celebrates is achieved and illustrated graphically in V, iii of the tragicomic version when a bed is introduced on the stage with the sleepy but satisfied Thersames and Aglaura on it. If the scene with the bed rolling on and off stage suggests to the modern reader a ridiculous television commercial for hide-away beds, Suckling himself must have thought the scene an effective and shocking *coup de théatre*. If harmonious love is the theme of the play, here is its illustration. The potentialities of the scene could no doubt be more fully realized after the Restoration with the advent of female actresses on the professional stage. In any event, Thersames and Aglaura in their bed must have made, if a cinematic cliché today, a lively scene in Suckling's time. The scene, however, in terms of public court life, would have been familiar enough, representing the necessary official viewing of a dynastic marriage.

Aglaura and Thersames once bedded, order is restored to the world. The King is forgiven and he forgives the Queen, only banishing her to "Diana's Nunnerie." Accord and harmony are achieved, and if the Platonic lady, Orithie, is mateless at the end, it is a proper fate as she herself sententiously declares:

> ORITHIE. Madam, I loved the Prince, not my selfe;
>   Since his vertues have their full rewards,
>   I have my full desires.
>   (V (c), iii, 194 - 96)

The tragic version, of course, ends in universal carnage precisely because Aglaura and Thersames don't make it to the marvelous bed. The scene might in some measure approach ritual, but it is difficult not to believe that Suckling's real interest is in dramatic shock, sheer staginess, and the hint of prurience.

Aglaura shows Suckling thoroughly at home with the theatrical conventions and themes of his day. If it is the play of an amateur, he is a highly gifted amateur. The flow of courtly talk, the witty dialogue, the skilled essays on current themes of conversation, the sense of lively scene all show real ability.

Aglaura represents a complete withdrawal from the actual world of Caroline England with its very real threats and challenges to a comfortable dream world of impossible dangers, spectacle, ornate and witty language, sex and sentiment. In one of the numerous debates in the play, Thersames describes the kind of consciousness that results in plays like *Aglaura:*

> THERSAMES. . . . . but if pleasures be themselves but dreames,
> What then are the dreams of these to men?
> That monster, Expectation, will devoure
> All that is within our hope or power,
> And ere wee once can come to shew, how rich
> Wee are, wee shall be poore,
>
> (III, ii, 106 - 11)

"That monster, Expectation," brings Aglaura and Thersames to bed because there is no hope; pleasures are but dreams. That sort of awareness demands *Aglauras.*

CHAPTER 4

The Plays: The Goblins and Brennoralt

I Romance: "a Pretty Plot . . . the Devils . . . and the Fighting"

THE date of Suckling's romance comedy, The Goblins, is
not exactly established. A reference in the play to Suckling's
own poem "A Sessions of the Poets" fixes the composition as not
before the autumn of 1637, while its appearance in a list of plays
belonging to the King's Men in 1641 supplies the outer date by
which it clearly was in existence.[1] Although it was revived a number
of times after the Restoration, knowledge of its stage history is
slight. Mrs. Knipp, an actress much admired by Samuel Pepys,
danced in it; and he saw the last two acts of the play, reporting that
it was "a play I could not make anything of by these two
last. . . ."[2]

It is not very likely he would have made much more of it had he
seen the play in its entirety. The Goblins is a confusing and chaotic
play; the characters hardly slow down enough to be identified, and
a goodly number of them are in disguise anyway. Like Aglaura it is
written so that individual scenes are more important than the
whole, but its action is less coherent and more episodic. Sir A. W.
Ward, writing in 1899, found it "a production which defies—and as
a drama hardly deserves analysis" and thought "the action . . .
perfectly bewildering."[3] More recently Ruth Wallerstein, in an essay pointing out Suckling's use of Shakespearean dramatic techniques in The Goblins, concurred with this view, calling the play
"almost chaotically disunified in tone and method."[4] The un-
doubted chaos of the play, however, may in large measure be attributed to its type. If it is also a silly play, it is not much sillier than
a Broadway musical. Its silliness, moreover, is somewhat mitigated

by a measure of wit and considerable stage liveliness.

No matter what is said in the play's defense, however, the action is undeniably confusing. The setting is Francelia at the end of a civil war. The Prince is in love with Sabrina, who is also loved by Samorat. Sabrina's brothers, however, unattractive young men called Philatell and Torcular, are opposed to Samorat's marital aspirations, preferring, for obvious political reasons, the Prince's candidacy. Their opposition is expressed dramatically as the play opens by their attempt to kill Samorat. Samorat is at a disadvantage until a stranger arrives on the scene, joins the fights, and evens the odds. It is later learned that the stranger, Orsabrin (his true identity unknown even to himself) is none other than the Prince's lost brother, who had been sent to safety at a dangerous point in the civil war between the Orsabrins and the Tamorens.

After some very busy fighting in which Samorat is slightly wounded and Torcular is presumed to have been killed by Orsabrin, the stage is cleared by the sudden appearance of a band of "*Theeves in Devils habits*" who chase off Samorat and Orsabrin and bind and carry away the wounded Torcular. A bit later Samorat informs Orsabrin that the thieves first appeared in the forest after the great battle between the Orsabrins and the Tamorens. They have patterned themselves somewhat after Robin Hood's band and entertain themselves by blindfolding their prisoners, carrying them off to their underground hideaway, forcing them to tell their life stories, and punishing or rewarding them according to their prisoners' merits. Given such occupations, it hardly comes as a surprise to find that the "Thieves" are, in fact, the remnants of old Tamoren's followers and are led by his younger brother, also called Tamoren. Moreover, the heir of the Tamorens, Reginella, an innocent girl modeled on Shakespeare's Miranda, lives with them, and, just as Tamoren intended her to do, falls in love with Orsabrin as soon as he is captured.

Such are the main outlines of the plot. The action involves the tying and untying of a series of narrative knots. Orsabrin and Samorat are taken prisoner, escape, and are taken prisoner again with astonishing rapidity. At last the proper recognition signs of romance are produced—"our Commission" and "the Diamond Elephant" (V, v, 166 - 67)—and the essential discoveries are made. The play ends with reconciliation and reunion. The marriage of Reginella and Orsabrin will unite the Tamorens and the Orsabrins; the civil war will be resolved. Sabrina will give the Prince another day to woo her, allowing Samorat and the Prince to stand as equal rivals.

Orsabrin has the last joyous word:

> A Life! a Friend! a Brother! and a Mistress!
> Oh! what a day was here: Gently my Joyes distill,
> Least you should breake the Vessell you should fill.
>
> (V, v, 285 - 87)

The space between the agonized beginning and triumphant conclusion has been filled with escapes, disguises, duels, mistaken identities, social satire, witty chatter, love-talk, a few songs, and a bit of
dance; in sum, a good deal of excitement and very little substance.

Both Prologue and Epilogue to *The Goblins* self-consciously
relate it to the work of earlier playwrights. They both claim for the
audience a modernity and sophistication unknown to the past.
Today's audience, the Prologue declares, is superrefined and
demanding:

> When *Shakespeare, Beaumont, Fletcher* rul'd the Stage,
> There scarce were ten good pallats in the age,
> More curious Cooks then guests; for men would eat
> Most hartily of any kind of meat;
>
> (123, 3 - 6)

and goes on to complain of the new demand placed on playwrights
for prologues and epilogues at a time when dramatic genius has
flagged:

> The richnesse of the ground is gone and spent,
> Mens braines grow barren, and you raise the Rent.
>
> (26 - 27)

The Epilogue claims "a pretty plot" for *The Goblins* and asserts
that if a fool had been added to the devils and the fighting, it all
would have been perfectly acceptable "and 't had bin just old
writing." But now, the Epilogue concludes, even the slightest and
least ambitious of plays will be critically torn apart by the supercen-
sorious audience:

> The ill is only here, that 't may fall out
> In Plaies as Faces; and who goes about
> To take asunder oft destroyes (we know)
> What altogether made a pretty show.
>
> (176, 21 - 24)

All this defensiveness may appear excessive and unwarranted; probably, however, it should just be seen as thoroughly conventional. The sense of the play's worth is nonetheless correct.

II *Shakespeare at a Distance*

"A pretty show" is finally just what *The Goblins* really is. Tamoren and his exiles vaguely suggest the Duke and his foresters in *As You Like It*. Sabrina mistakes Orsabrin for Samorat, a mistake highly pleasing to Orsabrin:

> Shees warme, and soft as lovers language:
> Shee spoke too, pretilie;
> Now I have forgot all the danger I was in.
> (II, i, 3 - 5)

The device is certainly not exclusively Shakespearean, but one is reminded of Sebastian happily mistaken by Olivia in *Twelfth Night*. Of course the most obvious Shakespearean parallel is to *The Tempest;* Reginella and Orsabrin are Suckling's version of Miranda and Ferdinand. Reginella asks at their first meeting:

> Tell me what thou art first:
> For such a creature
> Mine eyes did never yet behold.
> (III, vii, 79 - 81)

She is not even sure if she is a woman.

> I know not what I am,
> For like my selfe I never yet saw any.
> (III, vii, 90 - 91)

In such a play as this credulity cannot be strained, but Reginella's innocence frequently shades over into undeniable simplemindedness.

In fact Reginella reminds one perhaps less of Miranda than of Sir William Davenant's masculine parody of Miranda, Gridonell, a great booby in *The Platonic Lovers* who has been raised totally apart from women by a foolishly cautious father. This careful upbringing by no means induces the chastity for which the father had hoped, but the reverse. Reginella is perfectly well behaved, but that

she suggests Gridonell at all underscores the distance from
Shakespeare in *The Goblins*. Nonetheless the Shakespearean echoes
from *The Tempest* and other plays are clear and unmistakable. "I'le
ticke you for old ends of Plaies" (III, ii, 52), the wit Pellegrin cries,
and it is easy to see the game of literary allusion as part of the fabric
of the play. An outrageous exemplar is Orsabrin's parody of
Hamlet's most famous soliloquy:

> To die! yea what's that?
> For yet I never thought on't seriously;
> It may be 'tis. —hum.— It may be 'tis not too.—
> (III, iii, 1 - 3)

Orsabrin is in prison, his fortunes are at the ebb; the dramatic mood
has been that of romantic melodrama, not comedy, but it is hard to
imagine such lines not producing a roar of laughter from the
sophisticated audience. Suckling admired Shakespeare, but his admiration did not preclude parody; nor did his attitude toward the
materials of the play prevent him from deliberately shattering a
mood for the sake of a joke.

All this is not to say that *The Goblins* is essentially and consciously a parody of Shakespearean romance, but rather that the relation
of the play to Shakespeare is shifting and uncertain. Orsabrin breaks
into lyric celebration after meeting Reginella:

> But I'de carry thee where there is a glorious light,
> Where all above is spread a Canopie,
> Studded with twinckling Gems,
> Beauteous as Lovers eies;
> And underneath Carpets of flowry Meads
> To tread on.
> (III, vii, 98 - 103)

But Reginella cannot answer "O brave new world"; the world is too
palpably the same. The proposed marriage of Reginella and Orsabrin will settle the civil division of Tamorens and Orsabrins but
mechanically, with no larger overtones. The great Shakespearean
themes of reconciliation and rebirth are absent. Ultimately *The
Goblins* is no more Shakespearean romance than is John Fletcher's
version of *The Tempest, The Sea Voyage*. The imitation of
Shakespeare is finally limited to scenes, ideas, character types, in
sum to bits and pieces, not to the broader informing Shakespearean

spirit. When Samorat is arrested Philatell's response is to echo Othello:

> I'st ee'n so? Why then,
> Farewell the plumed Troops, and the big Wars,
> Which made ambition vertue.
>
> (IV, iii, 49 - 51)

The effect of the lines is to underline the distance of the dramatic world of *The Goblins* from Shakespeare.

Indeed, if one is to see the play as "something of what Shakespearean drama looked like to at least one intelligent courtier and gifted writer just before the closing of the theatres,"[5] the conclusion, then, must be that the surfaces were observed and not much more. The sensational and showy is caught, but there is no attempt to create the larger Shakespearean vision. Prospero's island and the whole world of Shakespearean romance supersedes reality because the metaphors are real and valid. The inadequacy of *The Goblins* as imitation of Shakespeare is the lack of overall metaphoric intent. The characters, the scenes, the action simply don't exist beyond their stage presence. Yeats's remark that "We should not attribute a very high degree of reality to the Great War"[6] might have puzzled Suckling, but it points to a fundamental difference between a minor artist like Suckling and a major artist like Shakespeare and to the limitations of *The Goblins*.

The Goblins is about the reconciliation of a postwar world. Francelia has suffered a civil war; the action of the play shows the resolution of the differences of the war. But it does so in an escapist fashion. It provides a momentary respite from the realities of the growing divisions in Charles I's kingdom and a facile vision of a happy ending. But the approaching war is always real, *The Goblins* only entertainment. The dream of *The Goblins* extends only to the immediate wish of the Caroline courtier for peace in his immediate political and social world. Prospero's island, on the other hand, is finally more real than the court to which he will return. *The Goblins* is "a pretty show," no more, no less. If its limits are recognized, its particular strengths can be more easily located.

III *Scene, Satire, and Song*

As with *Aglaura*, then, the strengths of *The Goblins* are with individual dramatic moments rather than with the design of the whole. The play opens with a duel; and sword fighting, wounds, and chases are never long absent. *"Flyes into the woods severall wayes pursued by Theeves in Devils habits"* (I, i) is a typical stage direction. Ardelan and Piramont are courtiers to whom young Orsabrin was entrusted in exile. When they are taken by Tamoren and the "thieves" in I, iii, a major bit of exposition is accomplished. The audience learns that young Orsabrin is alive, that he has been living (in proper romance fashion) with pirates, and that he is unaware of his true identity. But the exposition, important as it is, is clearly subordinate to the stage action. The "thieves" enter with Torcular to the sound of a horn. Torcular is taken off to a surgeon to have his wounds treated, and with more noise and bustle another entrance brings more thieves with more prisoners.

Tamoren welcomes them by singing:

> Bring them, bring them, bring them in,
> See if they have mortall Sin,
> Pinch them, as you dance about,
> Pinch them till the truth come out.
>   (I, iii, 7 - 10)

The song provides a stage direction for the ensuing stage business; and when Peridor hesitates, the direction is explicit, "Pinch him." The exposition is accomplished in some thirty lines and is followed by a second entrance of more of Tamoren's band, this time with a drunken poet in tow. The poet has no functional part in the play. In this scene he provides the opportunity for a drunken song with which to end the scene. He appears again in IV, v for some satirical treatment; it is likely that the poet is meant to be Ben Jonson and was so recognized by the court audience, but the direction of the satire is uncertain. The character exists in the play solely for his own independent possibilities for laughter and not for an integral dramatic purpose. In similar fashion in the scene just described the noise, the pinching, and the horseplay are finally more important than exposition.

The poet has just staggered off the stage when Orsabrin reappears, befuddled from having mistaken a bawdy house for a tavern. He is immediately set upon by a tailor and two sergeants who try to arrest him for debt. He drives them off, but is forced to flee himself when the constable and others arrive. He is chased from the stage and immediately reenters, this time in the garden of "a handsome house." The house is Sabrina's, and he is mistaken now for Samorat. When Orsabrin kisses Sabrina, she responds with Platonic delicacy, rebuking him for his "saucy heat." "S'foot!" he responds, " 'tis a *Platonique:* / Now cannot I so much as talke that way neither" (II, i, 15 - 16). This little topicality is really the center of the scene. It is no more than a light satiric touch, but it serves as a reminder that Francelia and the court of Charles I are not so distant; from time to time the wishful never-never land is converted into the more immediately recognizable. The central concerns of the play, however, are not with anti-Platonism or other court satire, but simply with entertainment.

"Oh you fill a place about his Grace, and keep out men of parts, d'you not?" (III, i, 19 - 20) surely expresses Suckling's own sour view of the court in which he was always outside the inner circle of power and influence. When Philatell urges the Prince to pretend that he will spare Samorat and then to execute him, he does so in terms that may reflect Sir John's continued bitterness over the disgrace of his uncle, the Earl of Middlesex:

> 'Tis but now owning of the fact,
> Disgracing for a time a Secretarie
> Or so—the thing's not new—
> (V, ii, 15 - 17)

The remark is a sharp critique of statescraft, but it, like the other satirical elements in the play, is essentially an aside. As was true with *Aglaura*, portions of *The Goblins* are essentially free-standing comic or satiric turns, doing nothing to advance plot or theme, but providing moments of fine language, wit, or topical commentary.

Nashorat and Pellegrin, the witty courtiers, discuss the virtues of country versus city women, a theme which will much engage the dramatists of the Restoration, and they do so in a fashion which forecasts the wit of Wycherly and of Congreve.

NASHORAT. 'Tis a rare wench, she 'ith blew stockings: what a complexion she had when she was warme—'Tis a hard question of these Country wenches, which are simpler, their beauties or themselves. There's as much difference betwixt a Towne-Lady, and one of these, as there is betwixt a wilde Pheasant and a tame.
PELLEGRIN. Right:—
There goes such essensing, washing, perfuming, dawbing, to th' other that

they are the least part of themselves. Indeed there's so much sauce, a man
cannot taste the meat.
NASHORAT. Let me kisse thee for that; by this light I hate a woman drest
up to her height, worse that I do Sugar with Muskadine: It leaves no roome
for me to imagine: I could improve her if she were mine: It looks like a Jade
with his tayle tied up with ribbons, going to a Fayre to be sold. (IV, iii, 1 -
14)

The dramatic prose skillfully conveys the sense of gentlemen talking. Their talk is on a set theme, a cynical variation on the praise of
simplicity and artlessness. Herrick comes quickly to mind, but the
artificial and the natural are skillfully combined to create the illusion of the "conversation of gentlemen" that Dryden so admired in
Suckling. Passages such as this represent what is perhaps the most
outstanding aspect of *The Goblins* and of Suckling's dramatic
achievement in general—that is, the creation of a truly effective
dramatic language capable of conveying the illusion of witty,
genteel conversation.
   The songs of *The Goblins* are undistinguished—two for pinching
and four for drinking—but they too, along with the dance in Act IV,
iii, are still another reminder of Suckling's sense of the play as a
series of sometimes discrete scenes and stage events. Nashorat's "A
health to the Nut browne Lasse," concluding:

> *She that has good Eyes,*
> *Has good Thighs,*
> *And it may be a better knack.*
> (III, ii, 87 - 89)

is the best in the play, a lively drinking song with a dash of bawdry.
   The Goblins, finally, does not show Suckling to advantage as a
serious writer of comedy. That is, *The Goblins* really has no enlarg-
ing thematic concerns. It is an entertainment and pretends to
nothing more. It is an escapist comedy wishfully looking to a
romantic world in which civil wars are resolved by forgiveness,
marriage, and returned princes. Behind it can be sensed a hard edge
of satiric feeling which unfortunately never emerges save in bits and
pieces. The reading of Shakespeare reduces him to moments of
parody and the broadest sort of imitation. *The Goblins*, considered
as sustained romantic and comic vision, is a failure, but its surfaces
are bright and shiny. Individual scenes are clearly the work of a
craftsman of no little skill and sometimes of real genius. Considered

on its own terms as "a pretty show," a mélange of stage excitement, song, and witty dialogue, *The Goblins* is a successful entertainment. Moreover, the closer *The Goblins* pushes to witty, quasi-realistic comedy, to the comedy of cynical, bright, conversational courtiers, in short to the sort of comedy to be most fully developed after the Restoration, the better it is. *The Goblins* does show that Suckling could turn out a perfectly competent and playable bit of stage entertainment, a claim that can't be made in all honesty for some other court playwrights and which indicates Sir John's healthy recognition of the demands of public stagecraft.

IV *The Tragic Voice:* Brennoralt

Brennoralt, Suckling's last play, shows his stagecraft even more to advantage. Admittedly *Brennoralt* is hardly a pleasing play by modern standards, but it reasonably well constructed, is filled with considerable action, and makes at least some attempt at distinctive characterization. It seems most likely that he wrote the play after nis return from Scotland and the First Bishops' War. The political and military allusions in it provide the play with additional historical interest. It is first mentioned under its alternate title, *The Discontented Colonel,* in a list of plays belonging to the King's Men, which were not to be published without permission.[7] On April 5, 1642, however, the publisher Francis Egglesfield entered *The Discontented Colonel* in the Stationer's Register and a quarto edition was published. Undoubtedly Egglesfield was anxious to capitalize on the play's topicality.

Although the substance of the plot is borrowed from Jean Pierre Camus's French romance *L'Iphigene,* published in Paris in 1625, and is set in Poland, Suckling clearly picked the story because of its application to the English scene; the rebellion of the Lithuanians against their Polish king obviously parallels the rebellion of the Scottish Presbyterians against their English king. Brennoralt, the discontented colonel of the title, is a conventional heroic soldier-lover in the tradition of Shakespeare's Antony and Chapman's Bussy d'Ambois. However, his topicality and even his rank, not nearly so elevated as that of his prototypes, suggest that he most probably represents a recognizable contemporary figure, perhaps Colonel George Goring, the daring, ambitious, and reckless cavalry officer, favorite of the queen, and governor of Portsmouth, who eventually betrayed the Army Plot to Parliament; or, even more

likely, Brennoralt may represent Suckling himself.[8] Whatever the
identification of the discontented colonel, the play moves between
extremes of realistic topicality and the fantasies of romantic tragedy.

V   The Plot: "Breasts! / By All That's Good, a Woman!"

The world of Brennoralt divides its attention, as does so much
Caroline drama, between love and war. Brennoralt, the discontented loyalist colonel, is in love with Francelia, the daughter of
the Pallatine of Mensecke, one of the leading rebels. Unfortunately
for Brennoralt, Francelia is betrothed to a gallant rebel officer,
Almerin. This rather standard romantic situation is complicated by
the presence of Almerin's friend, Iphigene, Pallatine of Plocence.
Not only is Iphigene on the loyalist side, but she is a girl disguised
as a man and has been so disguised all her life. She, of course, is in
love with Almerin; and given such a design, it is hardly surprising
that when she is taken prisoner by the rebels Francelia falls in love
with her. Although in Camus much is made of the possibilities for
smirking over transvestitism, Suckling ignores the opportunity and
handles Iphigene's peculiar circumstances decorously.

The play opens with a rebel attack on the royalists in which the
rebel Almerin is taken. Iphigene visits him in prison and laments in
pastoral fashion:

> O *Almerin;* would we had never knowne
> The ruffle of the world! but were againe
> By golden banks, in happy solitude;
> When thou and I, Shepheard and Shepheardesse,
> So oft by turnes, as often still have wisht,
> That we as eas'ly could have chang'd our sex,
> As clothes; . . .
>
> (I, iv, 1 - 7)

This speech underlines one of the major peculiarities of the play.
Almerin is unaware that Iphigene is a woman, knowing him / her
simply as a dear friend, their friendship being of that sort exalted by
so much Renaissance literature. No one, in fact, save Iphigene,
knows the truth of her identity. Her sex is revealed only in the last
act. Until that point there is nothing in the dialogue that would indicate to the characters or to the audience that Iphigene was a
woman in disguise unless the remarks of Almerin's lieutenant
colonel, Morat, and one of his soldiers are intended as a hint:

MORAT. Doest thinke he will fight?
SOLDIER. Troth it may be not:
　　　　　　　Nature, in those fine peeces, does as Painters;
　　　　　　　Hangs out a pleasant Excellence
　　　　　　　That takes the eye, which is indeed,
　　　　　　　But a course canvas in the naked truth,
　　　　　　　Or some slight stuffe.
MORAT. I have a great minde to taste him.
　　　　　　　　　　　　　　　　(III, iii, 22 - 29)

This would, as would many other moments in the play, supply substantial dramatic irony, but that irony can exist only at the expense
of surprise at the final revelation of Iphigene's true identity.
Suckling's audience may have been sufficiently aware of Iphigene's
story that they could chortle at appropriate moments, but the
ironies are not established by action or text. Consequently one can't
give Suckling overmuch credit for not making jokes about
transvestitism when the audience really doesn't have sufficient information to understand them.

　　When Almerin escapes and Iphigene is taken prisoner by the
rebels, the scene moves to the rebel fortress where Francelia immediately falls in love with Iphigene: "Would I had ne're seen this
shape, 't has poyson in't. / Yet where dwells good, if ill inhabits
there?" (II, iii, 27 - 28). When Brennoralt learns that Francelia is to
marry Almerin, his love drives him to the rebel
citadel—"Enough, / I am a storme within till I am there" (II, iv,
91 - 92)—where he manages to interview Francelia in her bed.
Brennoralt waxes eloquent and surprisingly reflective at the sight of
her sleeping beauty:

　　　　　　So Misers looke upon their gold,
　　　　　　Which while they joy to see, they feare to loose:
　　　　　　The pleasure of the sight scarse equalling
　　　　　　The jealousie of being dispossest by others;
　　　　　　Her face is like the milky way i' th' skie,
　　　　　　A meeting of gentle lights without name.
　　　　　　Heavens! shall this fresh ornament
　　　　　　Of the world; this precious lovelines
　　　　　　Passe with other common things
　　　　　　Amongst the wasts of time, what pity 'twere.
　　　　　　　　　　　　　　　(III, iv, 19 - 28)

All his eloquence wins him, however, is Francelia's declaration that she respects Brennoralt and does not love Almerin.

Brennoralt manages to get back to the royalist camp, and an assault is launched on the rebel fortress. In the midst of the royalist attack Almerin encounters Francelia and Iphigene together in a compromising situation. Francelia has just given Iphigene that popular love token of the Renaissance, a bracelet of her hair. In his jealous rage Almerin stabs Iphigene and Francelia. Iphigene, knowing she must die and believing that the truth should be told, confesses her sex. Almerin is understandably incredulous and with a furious "Ha, ha, ha, brave and bold!" (V, iii, 51) he charges at her again. Iphigene, however, is able to gasp out the sad truth that her father had threatened to abandon her mother unless she produced a male heir. After a succession of failures the desperate stratagem was adopted. The last girl, Iphigene, would be raised as a boy. Poor Iphigene concludes her pathetic tale and adds a further confession before she faints:

> If now thou findst that, which
> Thou thoughtst a friendship in me, Love, forget it.
> It was my joy,—and—death.
>
> (V, iii, 67 - 69)

Almerin goes to her aid and discovers conclusive proof of the truth of Iphigene's story:

> —Breasts!
> By all that's good, a woman!—*Iphigene.*
> (V, iii, 72 - 73)

Iphigene recovers from her faint to add a footnote to her story, explaining that she courted Francelia to keep Almerin from her. Almerin then confesses that throughout their long friendship he had often wished Iphigene were a girl and declares he would have loved her truly had she been a girl, instead of a boy, friend:

> Canst thou doubt that?
> That hast so often seen me extasi'd,
> When thou wert drest like woman,
> Unwilling ever to beleeve thee man?
> (V, iii, 87 - 90)

At last Almerin goes for a physician, but it is too late; Francelia dies.

Brennoralt and the royalist troops break into the room. He dismisses the soldiers and discovers the dead Francelia. He then kills Iphigene straightaway, assuming him / her to have been Francelia's murderer. Almerin returns and the two begin to fight, pausing only to kiss their dead loves:

ALMERIN. Even so have two faint Pilgrims scorch't with heat
        Unto some neighbour fountaine stept aside,
        Kneel'd first, then laid their warm lips to the Nymph
        And from her coldnesse took fresh life againe
        As we do now.
BRENNORALT. Lets on our journey if thou art refresht.
                              (V, iii, 224 - 29)

After this pretty and bizarre sentiment the heroes resume their combat until Almerin falls wounded. The king enters, and Almerin manages to explain the situation once more before he dies. The king, after appropriate acknowledgment of the peculiar and unhappy situation, turns to political matters to offer the victorious Brennoralt the forfeited possessions and titles of the leading rebels, but no note of happiness is allowed to intrude. Brennoralt refuses in terms that the audience would understand as referring to Charles I's own inept handling of rewards:

    A Princely gift! But Sir it comes too late.
    Like Sun-beames on the blasted blossomes, doe
    Your favours fall: you should have giv'n me this
    When't might have rais'd me in men's thoughts, and made
    Me equall to *Francelia's* love: I have
    No end, since shee is not—
    Back to my private life I will returne.
    Cattell, though weary, can trudge homewards, after.
                        (V, iii, 277 - 84)

A final melancholy word from the King and the play ends:

          . . . we have got
    The day; but bought it at so deare a rate,
    That victory it selfe's unfortunate.
                  (V, iii, 289 - 91)

VI   *Character, Politics, and Entertainment: "Real" Worlds*

Brennoralt certainly doesn't improve with the telling of it, but the same can be said of many plays. Dramatic representation can transform the silliest stuff. *Brennoralt*, we should recall, was successfully revived at the Restoration. Samuel Pepys saw it four times, once calling it "a good tragedy that I liked well."[9] Recognition that Suckling's plays were acceptable and more to his contemporaries may not help a modern reader to like them more, but it should at least cause the reader to ask what they found to admire and what Suckling was attempting in a play like *Brennoralt.*

Alfred Harbage's comment concerning *Brennoralt* that ". . . its political allusions are purely incidental; its heroic-romantic unreality makes it kin with typical Cavalier drama"[10] isolates two main factors which account for the play's success in its own time. The unreality which can seem too absurd to a modern reader was, after all, precisely what the Caroline audience wanted. One thinks of Van Dyck's equestrian paintings of King Charles—noble, elegant horses with monumental heads, necks, chests, and graceful, dainty legs that could never carry the weight of such a beast, and the king himself, handsome, refined, royal beyond all monarchal dreams. On the stage as in painting and in poetry, what mattered was not the realism of portrayal but its idealism and elaboration.

Brennoralt is nominally a tragedy, but the ending is contrived and not very well contrived. It depends totally on chance and circumstance. It has nothing to do with character; and finally, it evokes no particular response associated with tragedy. Indeed, the last major speech is given to Brennoralt, and it shifts the focus of the play from the deaths of Iphigene, Francelia, and Almerin to a contemporary political question, that is, the use and timing of royal rewards and favors.

Obviously the ending is no accident. Instead of concentrating on the deaths and reaction to the deaths, the high point of the play's ending has been in the duel of the two lovers and their tender first and last kisses. The tragic content has not mattered; the point is in the pose, the decoration, the elaboration of love found and lost—not on the emotion and meaning of the tragic finale, but on the manner. Brennoralt exits still discontented, still melancholy, his last words unequivocally returning the audience to the unheroic, unromantic realities of the court and the troubled politics of the day.

At this point one may ask to what extent the political allusions in *Brennoralt* are really "incidental." Suckling was attracted to Camus's *L'Iphigene* because of the potentials in the parallelism of the Lithuanian-Polish rebellion to the Scottish-English rebellion. The girl disguised as a boy is a device that is standard Renaissance fare, but Suckling does not seem much interested in the situation itself. It is a paradox upon which one may embroider and little more. There is no attempt to understand in any serious fashion the consequences of such a fate as Iphigene's. The possibilities for treatment of the major themes of appearance and reality are not exploited. Politics, then, may be incidental to the love story, but not to the play as a whole and not to Sir John's concerns. One might almost claim that the political allusions are the real heart of the play, the telling of the love story becoming merely the vehicle for political observations.

At any rate, it is not the plot per se that matters, but how the plot, traditional and familiar (in Caroline terms) as it is, is treated—how, in other words, it is ornamented. Iphigene and Francelia meet in the garden of the rebel fortress. Iphigene enters first, alone, and weeps, lamenting her fate and establishing the tone of the scene:

> Tempests of wind thus (as my stormes of griefe
> Carry my teares, which should relieve my heart)
> Have hurried to the thankelesse Ocean clouds
> And showers, that needed not at all the curtesie,
> When the poore plaines have languish't for the want,
> And almost burst asunder.—
> I'le have this Statues place, and undertake
> At my own charge to keepe the water full.
>
> (III, i, 10 - 17)

The concluding figure is a baroque commonplace, as Professor Beaurline points out, and can be found in poems by Donne, Jonson, and Marvell;[11] it is not too much to say that the scene almost exists in order to develop the figure. The passage emphasizes the formal, nearly emblematic quality, of the whole scene. Neither Iphigene nor Francelia is possessed of any qualities that might be identified as individual characteristics; so the scene cannot be and should not be viewed from the point of view of character. What remains is embellished language and a stylized presentation of incident.

The formal characteristics of the love story serve to set off and heighten the political commentary and certain realistic scenes. Brennoralt is a hard-liner, advocating stern measures against the Lithuanian rebels:

> If when great *Polands* honour, safety too,
> Hangs in dispute, we should not draw our Swords,
> Why were we ever taught to weare 'em Sir?
> (III, ii, 66 - 68)

The application to the Scottish rebels is clear enough. Miesla, one of the King's counselors, adopts the same contemptuous tone toward the issues of the war found in Suckling's letters:

> . . . . Religion
> And Liberty, most specious names, they urge,
> Which like the Bils of subtle Mountebankes,
> Fill'd with great promises of curing all,
> —Though by the wise,
> Pass'd by unread as common cosenage,
> Yet, By th' unknowing multitude they're still
> Admir'd and flock't unto.
> (III, ii, 74 - 81)

Clearly Suckling, always outside the real center of power in Charles's court, saw *Brennoralt* as a way of publicly stating his political views. Any fair reading of *Brennoralt* must admit its propagandistic function. All of the political allusions are greatly emphasized because they are set in an atmosphere of heroic and romantic ideality.

Similarly emphasized is the sparkling conversation of the witty and cynical Cavaliers under Brennoralt. These officers provide a genuine glimpse of the camp life of the Cavalier and offer a sharp contrast to the romantic fantasy of the heroic-love plot. In one of the liveliest, most brilliantly conceived scenes in the play, the Cavaliers engage in a drinking and extempore poetry contest.

> GRAINEVERT. Trouble not thy selfe, childe of discontent:
> 'twill take no hurt I warrant thee; the State is but a
> little drunke, and when 'tas spued up that that made it
> so, 'twill be well agen, there's my opinion in short.
> MARINELL. Th' art i' th' right. The State's a pretty
> forehanded State, and will doe reason hereafter. Let's
> drinke and talke no more on't.
> (II, ii, 1 - 6)

The great issues are casually dismissed; there is no point in worrying; they are soldiers, not thinkers. All one can do is drink and, as Grainevert does, sing:

> *Shee's pretty to walke with:*
> *And witty to talke with:*
> *And pleasant too to thinke on.*
> *But the best use of all,*
> *Is her health is a stale*
> *And helps us to make us drinke on.*
> (II, ii, 13 - 18)

The scene moves in sprightly rapidity with tags of Shakespeare, witty repartee, and song following song.

It is fine, lively theater, essentially the stuff of musical comedy, but above all it provides a sharp and welcome relief from the high-flown language and sentiment of the romantic-heroic plot. This is not to say that these insouciant Cavaliers are literally realistic portraits of Suckling's fellow royalists, but that this scene and others like it belong generically to realistic comedy. The carefree gaiety, the *sprezzatura* of the Cavaliers, moreover, establishes something of the court tone, if not the actuality, at least the kind of behavior and talk to which one might aspire. The two-sidedness of *Brennoralt* reflects the division of Cavalier society. The easy vacillation from witty, graceful cynicism and urbane disengagement to ornate, inflated heroic romanticism defines an inescapable aspect of the court of Charles I.

Still another opposition to the idealized romance of the main plot is found in the libidinous conversation of the Cavaliers. Their lubricity, however, avoids downright ribaldry and is transformed into high comic art, as when Grainevert eloquently embroiders on the theme of a beautiful young girl to his appreciative and increasingly randy companions:

GRAINEVERT. Ah—a sprightly girle about fifteen
That melts when a man but takes her by the hand!
Eyes full, and quick; with breath
Sweet as double violets,
And wholesome as dying leaves of Strawberries.
Thick silken eye-browes, high upon the fore-head;
And cheeks mingled with pale streaks of red,
Such as the blushing morning never wore—
VILLANOR. Oh my chops; my chops.
(IV,vi, 10 - 18)

The scene is pure interlude, an opportunity for elegant variations on themes of beauty and sex. It ends with news of approaching combat and a song by Grainevert in which he complains (again advancing one of Suckling's own views) of the disadvantages of a limited war and asks for unlimited and unrestricted warfare:

> *This moiety Warre,*
> *Twilight,*
> *Neither night nor day,*
> *Pox upon it:*
> *A storm is worth a thousand*
> *Of your calme;*
> *There's more variety in it.*
>   (IV, vi, 48 - 54)

With a song on their lips, then, the Cavaliers move off to battle, all pure pose, but political propaganda as well. The romantic idealism of the stance of the dashing Cavalier is oddly mixed with the serious political-military position Suckling advances in *Brennoralt*. Beyond all this, however, one can't help but admire the bright surface of the scene and its skillfully contrived illusion of reality.

VII   *Playwright-Courtier: Conclusion*

The three completed plays are, when all is said and done, a fairly substantial achievement when one considers that Sir John was an amateur playwright whose time was also occupied in military ex-peditions, court politics, and certainly gambling, drinking, and wenching. His talents were such that the professional playwright Richard Brome found it worth his while to satirize Suckling and Suckling's friend, Sir William Davenant, in *The Court Beggar*.[12] Both Suckling and Davenant were fair game for satirists for a var-iety of reasons, but Brome specifically includes Suckling's dramatic activities along with his gambling and abortive soldiering. That the professional should be sufficiently exercised over the playwriting of this elegant amateur to attack it is testimony to Suckling's skill and the threat he posed.

Aglaura is best seen as essentially spectacle, as a sort of overgrown masque, court entertainment. As such it made its splash and served the taste of the times. Both *The Goblins* and *Brennoralt* show a similar ability to meet the tastes of the day; Suckling knew how to write a play in the fashionable court manner. The manner is foreign and may be difficult for the modern reader to appreciate. The plays are written within a set of conventions, and modern theatrical conventions are at a considerable distance from those of the court of King Charles I. Artificiality, after all, is usually pejorative in the twentieth century, a connotative shift the seventeenth century would find surprising and almost incomprehensible. Suckling mastered the dramatic conventions of the day. He was able to create worlds of extravagant adventure, high romance, noble poses, and polished rhetoric. Within the conventions of Cavalier drama Suckling created the desired world of artifice to which one could retreat from the realities of increasing political and religious strife and from the daily commonplaces.

Beyond the mastery of the conventions of his day, he achieved something more that the modern reader can more directly and more sympathetically admire. He had a strong sense for the individual dramatic scene, for the theatrical moment, in particular for the comic turn, for the development of a joke, and for the setting of a song. This sense of the dramatic moment is closely linked with Suckling's distinct abilities for comic realism. When he writes heroic-romantic sentiment and bombast, Suckling sounds like a dozen other Caroline playwrights. On the other hand, when his Cavaliers chatter unbuttoned in tavern and camp, their dialogue is distinctive and brilliant. In those scenes, filled with song and witty conversation, Suckling's dramatic genius is found. His voice is the authentic voice of imagined gentlemen, urbane, artfully artless, wry, and humorous. Fine of itself, the realistic comic dialogue plays wryly against the heroic and romantic conventions. The aspects of Suckling's theater retained and admired by the Restoration were, of course, just that creation of the ideal conversation of gentlemen and the sureness of his comic touch. It is useless to speculate on his development as a playwright if he had not fled to France and died, if the war had not arrived, and if the theaters hadn't been closed, but at least one must recognize a substantial potential as a writer of social comedy. But *Brennoralt* was written in about 1640, and Sir John Suckling was dead a year later. As it is, in his three completed plays Suckling met his own standards of entertaining spectacle, wrote some brilliant comic scenes, and demonstrated a growing dramatic potential.

CHAPTER 5

Poems: Finding a Voice (1626 - 1632)

I *The Available Options*

IT is as a poet, of course, that Suckling is remembered and not as a dramatist or prose writer. If for most readers he is a vaguely recalled, briefly glimpsed figure gliding through the shadowy landscape of the Survey of English Literature, he is at least vaguely recalled fairly often and that recall frequently includes the memory of a poem or two. His reputation, for the general reader, is based on a few poems; and indeed, his total poetic output is not large. If the twelve poems Professor Clayton classifies as doubtful in his edition are excluded,[1] Suckling's poems are seventy-eight in number. Eleven of these are juvenile verses written around or before 1626.

Finally, however, the number of poems is irrelevant. Suckling's merits are not quantifiable, nor should they be measured against the scale of the works of grander, intenser, or more serious poets. Suckling was a serious craftsman and a conscious artist, but he did not publicly take himself seriously as a poet. He says quite the reverse in "A Sessions of the Poets":

> He loved not the Muses so well as his sport;
> And
> Prized black eyes, or a lucky hit
> At bowls, above all the Trophies of wit;
> (74, 76 - 78)

But the stance is a pose, the *sprezzatura* of the Cavalier poet. The poems are always "just a little something of my leisure moments." "I never drank of *Aganippe* well," said Sir Philip Sidney (Sonnet

96

74, *Astrophil and Stella*); "My tongue-tied Muse in manners holds her still," said Shakespeare (Sonnet 85), both in the sonnet convention, but the traditional device is similar. The denial becomes part of the poem.

No one will argue that Sir John Suckling is a major poet, but it can be claimed for Suckling, as Robin Skelton has cogently claimed for the Cavalier poets as a group, that: ". . . at a period when public events were overturning every established thing, when exile, civil war, revolution, and heresy were commonplaces of the time, the poets chose to reassert the primacy of the individual and the importance of ordinary human pleasure. Candid, witty, subtle, observant, sardonic, passionate, affectionate, and clear-headed, the poetry . . . remains a monument to human dignity largely because it chose to avoid pretension while delighting equally in both simplicity and sophistication."[2]

The denial of seriousness is paradoxically a part of what is Suckling's real seriousness, the avoidance of pretensions, the detachment, the humor, the witty civilization displayed in the poems. The poet who declares for black eyes and bowling in preference to the laureate wreath is not to be read for high seriousness and great feeling within the poems, but this is not to deny the ultimate importance of the poems. The disavowal of serious poetic intent does, however, establish critical limits and critical problems in approaching Suckling's poetry.

"The gate is open, and thy soule invited to a Garden of ravishing variety: admire his wit, that created these for thy delight . . ."[3] concludes the prefatory "To the Reader" of the first printed collection of Suckling's poems, *Fragmenta Aurea*, published by Humphrey Moseley in 1646. The reader opening this volume came first to a court poem, "On New-Years day 1640, To the King," an appropriate beginning for the posthumous volume of a loyal Cavalier. This public, occasional poem is followed by "Loving and Beloved," a spirited descant on a love theme. "There never yet was honest man / That ever drove the trade of love" (60, 1 - 2), its witty, brisk, colloquial opening would remind the reader of Donne and satisfy his expectations of Suckling's offhand, comfortably cynical, Inns of Court tone. The third poem, for which Clayton supplies the appropriate title, "Love's Offence," is hardly elegant, its wit adolescent, but the fashionable cynicism is unmistakable:

> Then thus think I,
>   love is the fart
>   of every heart:
> It pains a man when 'tis kept close,
> And others doth offend, when 'tis let loose.
>
>   (53, 14 - 18)

The fourth poem the reader found in the book was "A Sessions of
the Poets," a distinctly public, social poem, not so much literary but
social commentary, a poem positing a community of values, a clubby poem.

The impression gained by a quick glance at the first pages of
Fragmenta Aurea would be of a poet of surfaces, of wit, of manners,
of society. The impression needs qualifications and elaborations but
is essentially correct. The four poems do represent the basic options
within which Suckling chose to write. To these options of subject
matter—variations on love, wit-play, social, public poetry—another
choice is clear in the matter of expression. The immediate impression of these opening poems is of a simple and direct style, of,
moreover—a word impossible to avoid—*ease*.

The critical problem raised by this recognition is described by
L. A. Beaurline in the essay quoted in the first chapter. Critics lack
a vocabulary for simplicity. Beaurline helpfully points in that essay
to "Concerning Petty Poetry," the preface to *A Forest of Varieties*,
published in 1654 by an acquaintance of Suckling's, Lord Dudley
North. North may have written the preface as early as 1610; Suckling requested and presumably received a copy of the preface from
North, for in *A Forest of Varieties* Lord North prints a letter to
Suckling in which he describes the essay as "that peece which you
honored with your pretended conversion. . . ."[4] In "Concerning
Petty Poetry" North is primarily concerned with attacking the
"strong lines" and complexity of the sort of poetry we associate with
Donne and other "metaphysicals." North

cannot approve the ridling humour lately affected by many, who think
nothing good that is easie, nor any thing becoming passion that is not exprest with an hyperbole above reason. These tormentors of their owne and
their Readers braines I leave to be admired in their high obscure flight . . .
like ill ranging Spaniells they spring figures, and ravished with their extravagant fancies, pursue them in long excursions, neglecting their true
game and pretended affection. . . .[5]

He is all for clarity, ease, for "a naturall spirit and moving ayre (or accent)."[6] Dryden's famous observation in the *Discourse concerning the Original and Progress of Satire* that Donne "affects the metaphysics, not only in his satires, but in his amorous verses, where nature only should reign; and perplexes the minds of the fair sex with nice speculations of philosophy, when he should engage their hearts, and entertain them with the softness of love"[7] nicely expresses the view of Lord North who held that "verses of love should be verses of pleasure, & to please in love, the smoother the better."[8]

Suckling's general poetic position is certainly similar to that outlined by North in "Concerning Petty Poetry." Moreover, the title of the essay itself describes in the main what Suckling writes, "petty poetry," that is, the kind of poetry North describes as "mild as flowers unmedicinall for morality, meere Poseys or Nosegays, gay to the first sense. . . ."[9] North finds it necessary to defend "vaine pleasures": "For God being served and nature sustained, what fruit proceeds from our authority, learning, wealth, policy, and earnest intent to profit, but to satisfie our impulsive affections, which either propound to themselves a felicity whereof they faile in the possession, or seeke to divert by such imployments the dulnesse and otherwise obtruding miseries of their condition? which if you please to consider, you will the more excuse many pursuers of lawful and naturall delight, and value those pleasures at the better rate which are most perdurable and communicable."[10] Surely the position, even to its hint of underlying melancholy, was a congenial one to Sir John Suckling and describes rather accurately the aesthetic and intellectual stance of his poetry.

For North and for Suckling the Horatian formula that poetry should delight and instruct is shortened simply to delight. Whatever seriousness one may find in the poetry is not in intention but in attitudes beneath the surfaces. Suckling wrote his poems to circulate in manuscript among the court coterie; "publication" was in a reading, or, if musically set, singing. He would have been astonished at the idea of a solemn examination of his poems. Yet an examination of his poetry does reveal his considerable poetic merits and, for a start, how remarkably loveless these poems about love are.

II *Voiceless and Voiced*

The chronological ordering of the poems supplied in the Oxford

edition provides a useful, if arbitrary, way of approaching the
poems; moreover, the chronological arrangement does suggest the
main line of development in Suckling's poetry, a movement toward
his own distinctive poetic voice. The earliest poems are eleven
juvenile poems first discovered and printed by L. A. Beaurline.[11]
The religious and seasonal subject matter of these early poems is
one later abandoned by Suckling, but he did, of course, go on to
write An 'Account of Religion by Reason; and the antischolastic attitude expressed in "Upon St. Johns-day comeing after Christmas
day" is in agreement with that work:

> Let the Divines dispute the case, and try
> The dubiousnesse of that great mystery
> That *John* should live untill the day of doome:
> This may suffice, he stayes till *Christ* is come.
>   (10)

The epigram does not become a major form with Suckling, but the
epigrammatic style remains. "Upon Christmas" is an anti-
Puritanical poem in praise of traditional Christmas celebrations,
with a fine, Herricklike line envisioning Christmas games "with
spitts for speares, and dripping-pans for sheilds" (11, 8). The
traditional attitude is consistent with Suckling's later work, but the
subject matter is not repeated. "A Dreame" belongs to the tradition
of the religious dream poem. The poet dreams of the last judgment,
"Feareing the Bad, and yet expecting Good" (13, 8), and repents,
asking for God's pardon. Of more interest than the poem itself is the
reference to the Duke of Buckingham:

> Great Frends could nothing doe, noe lustfull Peere,
> Noe smooth-fac'd *Buckingham*, was *Favourite* heere.
>   (13, 17 - 18)

whose part in the impeachment of his uncle, the Earl of Middlesex,
Suckling so strongly resented. "A Dreame" with its double repeti-
tion of "meethoughts" may vaguely suggest Clarence's dream in
Shakespeare's *Richard III*. "But yet meethoughts it was too much to
dy" (13, 21) is slightly reminiscent of Clarence's "O Lord!
methought what pain it was to drown" (*Richard III*, I, iv, 21).
These early poems, perhaps some of them school exercises, show
Suckling's early poetic competence and his experimentation with

themes and poetic manners he would abandon for more congenial
subjects and style.

"A Dreame" is a traditional poem and so is the first of the secular
poems in the chronology, "His Dream." "His Dream" is the
secular, erotic version of the dream poem. The lover dreams
amorously of his mistress and awakes at a critical moment. The
poem is couched in traditional, lush language:

> I gaz'd a while on these, and presently
> A Silver-stream ran softly gliding by,
> Upon whose banks, Lillies more white then snow
> New faln from heaven, with Violets mixt, did grow.
> (15, 11 - 14)

It is essentially a voiceless poem which could have been written by
any moderately competent versifier of the period. So too might "A
Supplement of an imperfect Copy of Verses of Mr. Will.
Shakespears, By the Author," an imitation of stanzas in *The Rape of
Lucrece*, reflecting Suckling's admiration for Shakespeare. The imitation is very loose; what apparently attracted Suckling was the
conceited style of the poem. A title such as "Variations on Some
Shakespearean Poetic Conceits," would more appropriately
describe the poem. It is an experiment in a manner Suckling did not
develop.

Another trial run of no particular stylistic distinction is the bawdy
riddling poem, "A Candle":

> There is a thing which in the Light
> Is seldom us'd, but in the Night
> It serves the Maiden Female crew,
> The Ladies, and the Good-wives too.
> (19, 1 - 4)

Its bawdiness is certainly in Suckling's manner, but the verse is still
not distinctively Suckling's in style. Its continued popularity,
however, is attested by its appearance with a tune in four editions of
Wit and Mirth: or Pills to Purge Melancholy.[12] It is in a popular,
jocular, riddling vein, as are the three "character" poems which
follow it, "A Pedler of Small-Wares," "A Soldier," and "A Barber."
All of these verses depend upon rather heavy double-entendre; at
best they show Suckling's ability to toss off bawdy light verse. All of

the poems so far can be considered as steps in a search for style.

"Perjury disdain'd" is an admittedly slight poem, but the first in the chronological ordering that sounds a genuinely Sucklingean note and which presents one of the central themes of his poetry. Suckling even liked some of the lines so well that he used them with minor changes in *Aglaura;* additional parallels can be found in a letter to Mary Cranfield and in "Sonnet I."[13] The repetitions of theme and lines indicate not so much Suckling's poetic economy but that "Perjury disdain'd" represents a kind of home territory. The voice and the theme are repeated again and again because they are a central voice and theme.

> Alas it is too late! I can no more
> Love now, then I have lov'd before:
> My *Flora*, 'tis my Fate, not I;
> And what you call Contempt, is Destiny.
>   (21, 1 - 4).

The poem opens with the snap of conversation directly transcribed. The reader is in the midst of a little drama. Flora has been protesting the inconstant lover and his contemptuous lack of attention. But with a witty, casuistic argument he denies the charge. He is a mere victim of fatality and of the consequences of his own probity:

> . . . I have bound my self with oaths, and vowed
> Oftner I fear than Heaven hath ere allowed,
> That Faces now should work no more on me,
> Then if they could not charm, or I not see.
> And shall I break them? shall I think you can
> Love, if I could, so foul a perjur'd man?
> Oh no, 'tis equally impossible that I
> Should love again, or you love Perjury.
>   (7 - 14)

The argument itself is amusingly fallacious, but rests importantly on the implied drama of the poem. The speaking voice and the situation are both reminiscent of Donne; his "Womans Constancy," for example, is a casuistic argument for not loving in which the speaker credits the lady with intellectual subtleties which are his alone. The comedy of that poem is in large measure in imagining the lady's bafflement and rage at being credited with so abstruse an argument to her own undoing. So it is here with Suckling; the poem appears to compliment. Flora, one may imagine, is taken by the glitter of it, by the apparent logic, by the apparent compliment, and yet possibly furious at the insouciant contempt in the denial of contempt. The speaker has vowed "That Faces now should work no more on me" (22, 9), but "Faces" reveals the reductive, libertine attitude. Again and again Suckling will use "Faces" in this fashion; love is a matter merely of "faces," of the outward lure, nature's bright plumage. Finally, what must in the dramatic situation annoy the lady, the impertinence of the poem, the basic device of claiming the right not to be faithful out of a superior faith and out of her own honesty, establishes a major aspect of the speaker's wit, his heartless, detached, and airy superiority.

At this point it is well to return to L. A. Beaurline's essay, for from his reading of North, Beaurline goes on to Dryden and reminds us that Dryden valued Suckling for his courtly, gentlemanly conversational style—above all for his *urbanity*. Dryden cites Quintilian, and in Quintilian's *Institutes of Oratory*, as Beaurline says: ". . . urbanity means a talent for courtly writing and genteel conversation. He distinguishes it from rusticity, and describes it as a kind of politeness in words and accents and usage, having the taste of the town and even a tincture of erudition. . . . Then Quintilian lists certain subcategories of urbanity: saltiness, agreeableness, jesting, raillery, and elegant facetiousness."[14] This quality of urbanity is evident in "Perjury disdain'd"; and, in this poem in particular, the qualities of implied raillery and elegant facetiousness are paramount. The dramatic situation of the poem exists to create the pose of the speaker; and the pose is finally a social statement, an assertion of the urbane.

That same urbanity is even more brilliantly displayed in the witty modulations of tone in "Lutea Allison: *Si Sola es, nulla es.*" One meaning of *lutea* is "rose-colored" and the most obvious sense of the title is something like "Rosy Allison." Clayton, however, finds witty metonymic play in the title. He reads Allison as not just a girl's name but recalls that " 'Alison,' or 'Allison' (now Liesborn), was a Roman fortress built by Drusus near what was in Suckling's time the town of Wesel in the Spanish Netherlands."[15] Allison is then used metonymically for "fort" and *lutea* here is used with its meaning of clay or loam. The title then means "fort of clay," and so read suggests the popular Renaissance metaphor of seduction as siege and comments ironically on "Rosy Allison's" defensive capabilities. The motto, paraphrased in the poem as "One is no number, till that two be one" (25, 14) states the theme of the poem.

> Though you *Diana*-like have liv'd still chast,
> Yet must you not (Fair) die a Maid at last:
> The roses on your cheeks were never made
> To bless the eye alone, and so to fade;
>   (25, 1 - 4)

The language and the tone are all part of the familiar *carpe-diem* tradition; "One is no number, till that two be one" comes as a totally expected conclusion. The poet might have stopped there having satisfied the expectations of fourteen lines; instead the essentially decorous urgings to use nature's gifts "to love, to wed . . . for the Marriage-bed" (11 - 12) are abandoned in the remainder of the poem. The polite, almost prim and parsonical argument to marriage gives way to the goat-foot of the libertine:

> To keep a maidenhead but till fifteen,
> Is worse then murder, and a greater sin
> Then to have lost it in the lawful sheets
> With one that should want skill to reap those sweets;
> But not to lose't at all, by *Venus*, this
> And by her son, inexpiable is;
> And should each Female guilty be o' th' crime,
> The world would have its end before its time.
>   (26, 14 - 22)

If one thinks of the first fourteen lines as a sonnet and the last eight as its tail, Suckling uses the tail to reverse the intent and tone of the main body, to wag, in fact, the dog. The wit of the poem is in the sudden and surprising shift of tone, in the skillful dropping of one mask and the assumption of another. Suckling can't use the *carpe-diem* theme; it is not his mode; it is hardly urbane. He takes it up, enjoys our tolerant but bored acceptance of the familiar, then he drops the mask, the poem leers, and the poet has asserted his witty superiority to the reader and to an exhausted convention.

III   *Urbane Play: The Poet as Crocodile*

Of course this is play and Sir John is an extremely playful poet. The play is that sort described by F. J. Warnke as constituting an important element in baroque literature: "Agon and make-believe, two of the constituents of the play attitude, lead inevitably to that experience of almost vertiginous levity, of extravagant release, which one associates with the phenomenon of play. All three elements—agon, make-believe, and levity—are conspicuously present in Baroque literature."[16] And all are conspicuously present in much of Suckling's poetry. Warnke's general statement about play in baroque poetry, indeed, is at many points remarkably apposite to Suckling: "The playfulness of Baroque love poetry shows itself in four distinct but related features: the imposition of a double view, through which the speaker simultaneously voices his personal passion and distances himself from it in a half-amused way; the formulation of the speaker's relation to the beloved in quasi-dramatic terms; the use of comic hyperbole; and the practice of insulting or showing aggression toward the beloved, with the consequent creation of a kind of amorous agon, or erotic flyting."[17]

Illustration of a variety of the elements of urbane play can be found in the lines "Upon A.M." The basic maneuver of this poem is to reverse the *carpe-diem* theme; the lady is not to yield:

> Yeeld not, my Love; but be as coy,
> As if thou knew'st not how to toy:
> The Fort resign'd with ease, men Cowards prove
> And lazie grow. Let me besiege thy Love,
> Let me despair at least three times a day,
> And take repulses upon each assay.
>
> (27, 1 - 6)

The dramatic address, the implied aggression of the military metaphor are joined here by the paradoxical reversal of the seduction theme, but the apparent paradox is resolved by another paradox, this one sophisticated and in its way more libertine than any simple plea for the lady's compliance:

> Take no corruption from thy Grandame *Eve;*
> Rather want faith to save thee, then believe
> Too soon: For credit me 'tis true,
> Men most enjoy, when least they do.
>
> (13 - 16)

The poem argues for chastity, but for unchaste reasons. The comic play of "Upon A.M." rests in the reversal of values and is inten-

sified by the dramatic setting. Moreover, the tone is kept light, just
slightly superior and deftly taunting:

> If I but ask a kiss, straight blush as red
> As if I tempted for thy maidenhead.
>
> (7 - 8)

At one level of response the lines must produce a blush in the
dramatic audience, the imagined lady (or the real lady if one
assumes A.M. is more than a dramatic fiction), or an annoyed mock-
blush and a whisk of her fan and quite other reactions in the
sophisticated, worldly audience for whom the poem was written.
"Grandame *Eve*" belongs to the language of travesty; it is reductive, cheerfully contemptuous. The Fall of Man becomes a comedy,
Eve and all women become comic figures. All sexuality, all passion
is rendered absurd because of the libertine perception asserted by
the poem. Keats's figures on the Grecian urn forever wooing yield
pathos and a tragic awareness. The awareness for Suckling, lurking
in the background, unstated and certainly not to be pursued, is dark
and almost despairing.

Looked at too closely, "Upon A.M." is profoundly cynical, but it
is not to be looked upon that closely. It is, after all, a joke. Nor can
one read it with any pleasure if compelled to dwell upon the implicit attitude toward women in the poem. It is a variation upon a
theme. Love poetry is usually concerned with fruition, but the
traditions of Platonic love provided a basis for a sort of antifruition
poetry which rested on the doctrines of superior spiritual love.
Suckling's antifruition poems mock both the Platonist and the ordinary lover; he mocks them with the pose of a superior libertine, a
sexual gourmet.

The urbane poet delights in reversals, in surprising expectations,
in quietly and deftly turning things upside down and in being able,
once having displayed the legerdemain, to stand aside and grin at
the reader just a little. "A Song to a Lute" is that sort of poem. It is
a parody of the third stanza of the section called "Her Triumph" in
Ben Jonson's "A Celebration of Charis in Ten Pieces." Jonson's
poem first appeared in print, however, in 1631 as a song in his play
The Devil is an Ass. Suckling also intended "Song to a Lute"
dramatically, placing it in the unfinished play, *The Sad One.*
Beaurline suggests that the song circulated separately from the
play,[18] and undoubtedly he is correct.

Jonson's song is a little masterpiece, and so, in its own right, is the
stanza Suckling parodied:

> Have you seene but a bright Lillie grow,
>   Before rude hands have touch'd it?
> Ha' you mark'd but the fall o' the Snow
>   Before the soyle hath smutch'd it?
> Ha' you felt the wooll of Bever?
>   Or Swans Downe ever?
> Or have smelt o' the bud o' the Brier?
>   Or the Nard in the fire?
>   Or have tasted the bag of the Bee?
> O so white! O so soft! O so sweet is she![19]

Its simple lushness, the inevitability of its design, its intensity and
implicit poignancy represent a kind of absolute in the love lyric.
The soft tones of the lute, the melancholy tension of the
countertenor voice, flickering candlelight—it is not difficult to imagine the scene—and the ladies touching away an embarrassed tear
at the song. In the context of *The Devil is an Ass*, of course, the
song is a workaday seduction lyric, but dramatic contexts disappear.
It is finally a pretty, delicate, and sentimental song.

> Hast thou seen the Doun ith' air
>   when wanton blasts have tost it;
> Or the Ship on the Sea,
>   when ruder winds have crost it?
> Hast thou markt the Crocodiles weeping,
>   or the Foxes sleeping?
> Or hast view'd the Peacock in his pride,
>   or the Dove by his Bride,
>   when he courts for his leachery?
> Oh so fickle, oh so vain, oh so false, so false is she!
>   (29, 30)

Suckling's parody is quite as pretty a song; the mimicry of sound
and design is deft and exact. The reversal of tone and effect is complete. It is not that Sir John has created a gargoyle; the song is too
light, too quick and airy for that, but there is something of the antimasque to Jonson's masque—crocodiles, foxes, peacocks, and
lecherous doves (a *Volpone*-like bestiary) mock Jonson's elegant vision. But the mockery is eminently civilized; the possibility of

bitterness is avoided because of the civilization; fickle, vain, and false, but it is all quite amusing, elaborate, elegant, courtly teasing.

Of all of Suckling's poems belonging to this period the finest, wittiest, and most distinctively voiced is "Upon my Lady Carliles walking in Hampton-Court garden." In the version published in *Fragmenta Aurea* it is successfully playful; the manuscript version, as shall be suggested later, is less so. Lucy, Countess of Carlisle, was a daughter of the ninth Earl of Northumberland and the second wife of James Hay, the first Earl of Carlisle; beautiful and witty, she was celebrated in verse by Sir William Davenant, Edmund Waller, Robert Herrick, Thomas Carew, and others. "Upon my Lady Carliles walking in Hampton-Court garden" is written as a dialogue between T. C. and J. S., Thomas Carew and John Suckling. The dialogue establishes not just two attitudes toward the countess but also varying attitudes toward complimentary love poetry and sexuality. The wit of the poem is in the brilliant play of polarities and in the amused conversational tone or tones, because the dialogue offers, as it were, poetic and conversational options.

Against Carew's polished, elegant voice of courtly (and by implication, Neoplatonic) compliment Suckling sets his own raw, cynical, libertine, and predatory bark. It is masque and antimasque again or perhaps mask and unmask, for by the fifth stanza Carew's elegant tone has been modulated to suggest the libertine.

> Didst thou not find the place inspir'd,
> And flow'rs, as if they had desir'd
> No other Sun, start from their beds,
> And for a sight steal out their heads?
> Heardst thou not musick when she talk't?
> And didst not find that as she walkt
> She threw rare perfumes all about
> Such as bean-blossoms newly out,
> Or chafed spices give?
>
> (30, 1 - 9)

This is Carew's voice opening the poem and setting the argument and it is the very voice of Caroline high poetry, the idealization of the court lady, the essence of compliment and romantic aspiration. But Suckling replies in the negative in the next stanza, "I must confesse those perfumes *(Tom)* / I did not smell . . ." (10 - 11), and provokes Carew's indignant response:

> Dull and insensible, could'st see
> A thing so near a Deity
> Move up and down, and feel no change?
>
> (31, 18 - 20)

But the Suckling of the dialogue is not going to play literary games. His response is blunt and naturalistic and witty:

> None, and so great, were alike strange;
> I had my Thoughts, but not your way,
> All are not born (Sir) to the Bay;
> Alas! *Tom,* I am flesh and blood,
> And was consulting how I could
> In spite of masks and hoods descry
> The parts deni'd unto the eye;
> I was undoing all she wore,
> And had she walkt but one turn more,
> *Eve* in her first state had not been
> More naked, or more plainly seen.
>
> (21 - 31)

The maneuver is that of the dramatist introducing a realistic voice in the midst of artificiality, as if, say, in Walter Montagu's *The Shepheard's Paradise* someone suddenly stopped speaking nonsense. Within the poem the effect is to shift the mode of compliment; Lady Carlisle is seen not as a goddess of one tradition of love poetry but as the desirable sexual object of another. Outside the poem, or within the dramatic or theatrical device of the poem, the effect is similar to that when one actor is deliberately "broken up" and forced to "blow his lines" by another. The Tom Carew of the poem, confronted by J. S.'s frank and unpoetic reply, drops his mask, loses his courtly voice, and responds naturalistically as a fellow libertine:

> 'T was well for thee she left the place,
> For there's great danger in that face;
> But had'st thou view'd her legg and thigh,
> And upon that discovery
> Search't after parts that are more dear,
> (As Fancy seldom stops so near)
> No time or age had ever seen
> So lost a thing as thou hadst been.
>
> (32 - 39)

The "play" in the poem is a double one. The Carew of the poem is forced to drop his polite courtly pose and accept the libertine values and voice of the Suckling of the dialogue, to admit, in other words, his own libertinism. The easy, chatty "Alas! *Tom*, I am flesh and blood" with its comfortable familiarity and unabashed unwillingness to indulge in the language of court Platonism even for a moment, J. S.'s almost obstinate unwillingness to be "poetic" has forced T. C. to give up his pretensions and descend to a naturalistic world where girl-watching, even of countesses, is sexual rather than spiritual. Secondly the poem takes on a new character as compliment. What began as fleshless idealization is now bawdy; its bawdiness, however, is tempered by the cleverness of the modulations and by the distancing effect of the dialogue itself, by our sense of a little drama; it is all not to be taken too seriously. The movement of the poem is toward impudence and impertinence—in Warnke's phrase, "erotic flyting."

The text of the poem printed in *Fragmenta Aurea* extends this far, and if one makes allowances for a certain roughness, might still be considered compliment, if slightly left-handed. It may be preferable to be a goddess, but to be praised as sexually desirable is still something, and the latter praise may be far more honest than the former. A final stanza found in manuscript and printed for the first time by Thomas Clayton in his edition, however, changes the whole tone of the poem from dubious compliment to certain insult and a more cynical wit. Instead of letting the poem end with Carew's admission of the countess's sexual merits, J. S. is given the last word, an indecent and insulting amplification on that theme:

> 'Troth in her face I could descry
> No danger, no divinity.
> But since the pillars were so good
> On which the lovely fountain stood,
> Being once come so near, I think
> I should have ventur'd hard to drink.
> What ever fool like me had been
> If I'd not done as well as seen?
> There to be lost why should I doubt,
> Where fools with ease go in and out?
>   (31, 32; 40 - 49)

The last stanza turns Lady Carlisle into a whore who consorts with fools; the language would hardly please the lady or her husband,

James Hay, Earl of Carlisle. The omission of the stanza from the
poem as printed in *Fragmenta Aurea* may have been because of the
indecent libel contained in it. The stanza does, however, formally
round off the poem. Suckling has the last word and there is an
ironic reversal in which T. C.'s blunt references to "legg and thigh"
and "parts that are more dear" are transformed into the poetically
circumlocutious "pillars" and "lovely fountain." The additional
stanza strengthens the formal symmetry of the poem and increases
the "flyting" quality of it.

The coarseness of the stanza provides a link to the witty, good-
humored, and ribald "Upon T. C. having the P." Once again T. C.
is Thomas Carew; the "P" is the pox, the poem being one of those
jokes about syphilis which the age found so amusing. To call it a
poem about love may appear archly ironic, but the blunt consciousness of such venereal consequences contributes to the subterranean darkness of Suckling's poetry; at the least the awareness
serves to qualify any temptation toward romantic Petrarchanism.
The poem is slight, conversational, offhand:

> Troth, *Tom*, I must confess I much admire
> Thy water should find passage through the fire.
> (32, 1 - 2)

The opening lines set the tone and establish the conceit. The pox is
one of those little contretemps gentlemen will encounter. The juxtaposition of this poem with "Upon my Lady Carliles walking in
Hampton-Court garden" is the consequence of modern editing, the
former first appeared in print in 1659 in *The Last Remains* while
the latter was first printed in the 1646 edition of *Fragmenta Aurea;*
still, "Upon T. C. having the P." provides an amusing commentary
to T. C.'s poeticisms in the first stanza of "Upon my Lady Carliles
walking in Hampton-Court garden."

Two final poems belonging to the period from 1626 to 1632 illustrate Suckling's use of other poetic voices. Both "The deformed
Mistress" and "Detraction execrated" are less successful than even
"Upon T. C. having the P." They are so because they are less
genuinely urbane and because they are so clearly exercises in genre
and lacking in a distinctly personal voice. Both, however, do indicate poetic options open to Suckling, options which he briefly exercised.

"The deformed Mistress" belongs to the tradition of the "praise

of ugliness" of which John Donne's "The Anagram" is a far
superior example. Donne argues the paradox from a workable
proposition, "Love built on beauty, soone as beauty, dies"[20] and the
wit of "The Anagram" is in the play of wilfull paradox and valid
argument. Suckling instead simply asserts a whim:

> Each man his humor hath; and faith 'tis mine
> To love that woman which I now define.
> (33, 7 - 8)

The poem then proceeds with the definition by advancing one nasty, ugly image after another:

> Her Nose I'de have a foot long, not above,
> With pimples embroder'd, for those I love;
> And at the end a comely Pearl of Snot,
> Considering whether it should fall or not:
>
> . . . .
> As for her Belly, 'tis no matter, so
> There be a Belly, and a Cunt below;
> Yet if you will, let it be something high,
> And always let there be a timpanie.
> (33, 13 - 16; 34, 27 - 30)

The poem has a degree of Rabelaisian gusto, but isn't really one of
his better efforts. Suckling abandons the rationale for the paradox
and thereby the opportunity for real wit. The poem shows Suckling
yielding to the temptation to be coarsely naughty. To claim on the
basis of this poem, however, that he was personally misogynous is to
ignore the tradition which spawned the poem.

"Detraction execrated" is a more attractive poem than "The
deformed Mistress"; yet it too belongs to an established tradition
and shows Suckling speaking in a voice other than his own. The
genre is that of the "curse" or "imprecation." Donne's "The
Curse" is of the same type, but it provides only a distant model.
Nonetheless, the voice of "Detraction execrated" is modeled after
Donne's:

> Whence hadst thou thy intelligence, from earth?
> That part of us ne'r knew that we did love:
> Or from the air? Our gentle sighs had birth
> From such sweet raptures as to joy did move:
> Our thoughts, as pure as the chaste Mornings breath,

> When from the Nights cold arms it creeps away,
> Were cloth'd in words, and Maidens blush that hath
> More purity, more innocence then they.
>
> (35, 9 - 16)

The poem implies drama, even if the person addressed, "vermin
Slander," is an abstraction. The series of questions and answers, the
implied dialectic of the poem, convey an intensity reminiscent of
Donne, as does the poem's intellectualized structure provided by
the formal movement through the elements of earth, air, fire, and
water. The Platonism of the stanza just quoted, of lines like,

> Whilst our two souls in amorous extasie
> Perceiv'd no passing time, as if a part
> Our Love had been of still Eternity.
>
> (35, 22 - 24)

(an echo of Donne's "The Extasie"), belong to a tradition and style
alien to Suckling, but which he imitates with real competence.
"Detraction execrated" shows once more Suckling's technical skill,
but is uninteresting as a poem because it is so clearly imitative, so
completely uninhabited.

From this survey of a sample of the twenty-seven poems belonging to the years from 1626 to 1632 one can see Suckling writing in a
variety of styles and using a number of poetic conventions. Further,
one can see the startling difference between the conventional,
voiceless, imitative poems and those in which Sir John finds and
speaks in his own personal, distinctive voice, when he stops practicing and imitating.

> Expect not here a curious River fine,
> Our wits are short of that: alas the time!
> The neat refined language of the Court
> We know not. . . .
>
> (28, 1 - 4)

Suckling apologizes in "A Prologue of the Author's to a Masque at
Wiston." The poems up to 1632 show well enough that the dis-
claimer is false, a pose. He was in full command of the "neat refined language of the court," but it was not his own language and
not the voice he wanted. That voice is clearest when he approaches
the conventions at a distance and uses them ironically and urbanely.

Suckling writes his best poetry on matters of love and is most himself when he puts himself at odds with the conventions which had so long dominated Renaissance love poetry. Suckling's sense that it is the end of the line for a whole tradition leads him, finally, to his own distinctive voice and to a poetry that derives its merits from its attempts less to use than to mock the old attitudes and traditions.

CHAPTER 6

Poems: The Poet as Lover
(1632 - 1637)

I To Love or Not to Love

B ETWEEN 1632 and 1637 Suckling lost his entire patrimony
of some £7,000, unsuccessfully courted Anne Willoughby in
hopes of a profitable marriage, was cudgeled by Sir John Digby,
was involved in numerous lawsuits, spent a few days in jail for
brawling, met and courted Aglaura, and may have invented cribbage.[1] Except for Aglaura, nothing in this catalogue points to a
deeply romantic temperament. In the same period, following
Clayton's dating of the poems, Sir John wrote thirty poems. All of
them are "love" poems or poems having aspects of love for their
themes; but nothing in the poems, it must be added, points to a
deeply romantic temperament either. The range of the poems is
quite narrow, but they show Suckling in complete control of his
poetic material. He has mastered the conventions of traditional love
poetry and has achieved his own wry, witty, and urbane voice, a
voice which effectively mocks the traditional conventions.

Of the thirty poems of the period eleven can be classified as
written within the traditional conventions. "The Invocation," for
example, concludes:

> To love, or die, beg only I,
> Just Powers some end me give;
> And Traitor-like
> Thus force me not
> Without a heart to live.
> (45, 21 - 25)

The speaker, the tone, the subject all belong to the Petrarchan

tradition. It is a perfectly adequate poem and perfectly conventional. "The Expostulation I" is an oddity because, along with the
translation "Disdain," it is one of only two poems by Suckling in
which the fictional speaker is a woman. The oddity of the poem,
however, ends with the fact of the feminine persona. What the lady
has to say is familiar enough. She will love her *Coridon* even if he is
above her and she defies all her critics. These poems and nine more
can be classified as working within the basic conventions of love
poetry, of accepting both the literary conventions and love itself as
positive values. With few exceptions (certainly "To his Rival II"
and the "Song," "No, no faire Heretique") these poems which
accept the conventions are of mediocre quality, able but finally
lifeless.

The poetry becomes lively as soon as it is at odds with the conventions, when it seems to bear some relation to the dissolute,
rakehell realities of Suckling's own life. The theme which runs
through all this poetry is stated in the two opening poems, both
"Against Fruition." Both develop the same paradox and belong to
the tradition of the paradox poem. As with "Upon A.M." the argument against fruition is that love can only be a disappointment; the
greatest pleasure is in the imagination, in expectation.

> Stay here fond youth and ask no more, be wise,
> Knowing too much long since lost Paradise;
> The vertuous joyes thou hast, thou would'st should still
> Last in their pride; and would'st not take it ill
> If rudely from sweet dreams (and for a toy)
> Th'wert wak't? he wakes himself that does enjoy.
>
> (37, 1 - 6)

The opening of "Against Fruition I" is direct and colloquial in its
rhythms; again Suckling implies a little drama, the colloquy
between the young lover and the older wise counselor. The "fond
youth" is fond because foolish and foolish because fond. The states
are mutually inclusive. The amused irony is established in the first
line and furthered by the deft twist of the second. The speaker in
essence cites scripture, but he cites it paradoxically. The wisdom he
offers is that of the old roué who knows that "even kisses loose their
tast" (12).

In the third stanza the counselor responds to the youth's familiar
argument for the reproductive necessity of fruition:

> Urge not 'tis necessary, alas! we know
> The homeliest thing which mankind does is so;
> The World is of a vast extent we see,
> And must be peopled; Children then must be;
> So must bread too; but since there are enough
> Born to the drudgery, what need we plough?
>
> (13 - 18)

The lines give another twist to the joke. Antifruition arguments are the territory of fashionable court Platonists, but, as has been seen, the speaker of the poem usurps their place with a disreputable, hedonistic, libertine argument. Next, he adopts or parodies their absurd, snobbish, superrefined, hyperaristocratic posturing. Suckling repeats essentially the same gibe in *Aglaura* when the Platonic Orithie asks the fleshly Orsames in horror:

> Will you then place the happinesse, but there,
> Where the dull plow-man and the plow-mans horse
> Can find it out?
>
> (I, v, 16 - 18)

The joke was in the air and the precious affectations of court Platonism got the ridicule they deserved. In the last two stanzas the speaker drops the aesthetic pose and returns to the central thesis that " 'Tis expectation makes a blessing dear" (38, 23).

"Against Fruition II" expounds the same theme. It is less clearly dramatic:

> Then fairest Mistresse, hold the power you have,
> By still denying what we still do crave:
> In keeping us in hopes strange things to see
> That never were, nor are, nor e're shall be.
>
> (39, 23 - 26)

The mistress addressed in the conclusion is more general than specific, but the poem does nonetheless open with a vigorous "Fye upon hearts that burn with mutual fire" (38, 1) and the illusion of speech. The tone of "Against Fruition II" is darker than the preceding poem and more broadly antifeminine:

> Shee's but an honest whore that yeelds, although
> She be as cold as ice, as pure as snow:

> He that enjoys her hath no more to say
> But keep us Fasting if you'l have us pray.
>   (38, 19 - 22)

The final couplet illustrates a rather forced and dislocated quality in the poem, its failure as argument. "Fruition II" is finally a poem of moments, of wit lodged in individual lines rather than in the whole work, a criticism applicable to many of Suckling's less successful poems.

The parodies of these two poems by Edmund Waller and Henry Bold point to their popularity and to the currency of the theme. Both parodies attempt a libertine refutation, but neither one really quite works as a response to Suckling's antifruition arguments because the paradoxical libertine position that pleasure is greatest unconsummated can't be refuted by a simple denial on standard libertine grounds. On the other hand, Suckling does not argue just on libertine grounds. Both poems share the view expressed in "Against Fruition II" that:

> That monster Expectation feeds too high
> For any Woman e're to satisfie:
>   (38, 15 - 16)

Cynicism is, after all, disappointed idealism, and a certain poignancy lurks in the ostensible misogyny. The poems are difficult to parody because they are more complex than they appear. Their complexity results from a playful shifting of values, a multiplicity of attitudes.

Play between contradictory positions is seen in the pair of poems "To Mr. Davenant for Absence" and "Against Absence." The first is an answer to a poem attributed to William Davenant, "To Mr. W.M. Against Absence." Clayton places the poem among Suckling's dubious poems and concludes that "of all the dubious poems, this one, . . . has the strongest claim to his authorship."[2] On the other hand, "To Mr. W.M. Against Absence" was printed in Davenant's *Works* in 1673. At any rate, taken together the three poems illustrate the pleasure taken in developing themes and counterthemes, in thematic volleying.

> You vainely take the Paynes to fly from her
> On whom in absence you do ever thinke,
> For that's a kind of seeing when you winke.
>   (94, 16 - 18)

"To Mr. W.M. Against Absence" concludes with an epigrammatic
and proverbial bite. The concluding volley of "To Mr. Davenant for
Absence" is sharper:

> Love is a fit, and soon is past,
> Ill dyet onely makes it last;
> Who is still looking, gazing ever,
> Drinks wine i'th' very height o'th' Fever.
> (39, 17 - 20)

The game gets still livelier with the next variation developed in
"Against Absence":

> My whining Lover, what needs all
> These vows of life Monastical?
> Despairs, retirements, jealousies,
> And subtile sealing up of eyes?
> Come, come, be wise, return again,
> A finger burnt's as great a pain."
> (39, 40; 1 - 6)

The target is directly specified, the colloquial, argumentative quality is increased. The impatient speech rhythms of "Come, come, be
wise" sharpen the dramatic sense of the poem.

> Return then back, and feed thine eye,
> Feed all thy sences, and feast high.
> Spare dyet is the cause Love lasts,
> For Surfets sooner kill than Fasts.
> (40, 33 - 36)

The conclusion again carries the authority of proverbial wisdom (a
favorite device of Suckling) and an ironic play on the theme of fruition. The remedy for love is love.

The pair of poems "To his Rival I" ("My dearest Rival, least our
Love") and "To his Rival II" ("Now we have taught our Love to
know") again vary the fruition theme. This time, in "To his Rival
I," the rivals are to devote their time to praising the beloved:

> Impossible shall be our hope;
> And Love shall onely have his scope
> To join with Fancy now and then,
> And think what Reason would condemn:

> And on these grounds wee'l love as true,
> And if they were most sure t'ensue;
>   (41, 11 - 16)

and lack of fruition becomes a source of poetic inspiration.

> Mean time we two will teach our hearts
> In Lovers burdens bear their parts:
> Thou first shalt sigh, and say shee's fair,
> And I'le still answer, past compare;
> Thou shalt set out each part o'th' face,
> While I extol each little grace;
> Thou shalt be ravisht at her wit,
> And I, that she so governs it;
> Thou shalt like well that hand, that eye,
> That lip, that look, that majesty;
> And in good language them adore:
> While I want words, and do it more.
>   (41, 19 - 30)

The variations of tone are light-handed but subtle. Love becomes only literary, the domain of fancy. Literary license allows what reason condemns. The pun on "Lovers burdens" increases the wry, sardonic note. The burdens are musical refrains and musical parts but the sufferings of lovers as well. The Rival in Petrarchan fashion sighs and the Speaker with tongue-tied modesty echoes, "past compare." The divisions of praise are innocuous in the next couplet, but the wryness returns with the ambiguity of the Speaker's surprise that the lady can control her wit. The Rival adores in "good language," "While," says the Speaker, "I want words, and do it more." The quality of the rivalry here suggests the dichotomy earlier found in "Upon my Lady Carliles walking in Hampton-Court garden." The hints of other values, the suggested drama, the witty play of the language,

> Thus will we do till paler death
> Come with a warrant for our breath
>   (41, 35 - 36)

with *paler* playing on the paleness of the Petrarchan lover, all contribute to the inventive complexity of the poem within a framework of ostensible simplicity.

In "To his Rival II" Suckling imagines a shared love kept alive because the lady both love shares the antifruition doctrine:

> She then by still denying what
> We fondly crave, shall such a rate
> Set on each trifle that a kisse
> Shall come to be the utmost blisse.
> (42, 13 - 16)

In another context or culture the lady would be a tease; but here, for in this poem Suckling accepts the conventions and writes within the fiction of court Platonism, the lady (rather oddly called Desdemona, a name also used in letter No. 50, To T. C.) is an ideal. She won't be obvious or in any way ordinary:

> But ev'ry smile and little glance
> Shall look half lent, and half by chance:
> The Ribbon, Fan, or Muffe that she
> Would should be kept by thee or me,
> Should not be giv'n before too many,
> But neither thrown to's when there's any;
> So that her self should doubtful be
> Whether 'twere fortune flung't, or she.
> She shall not like the thing we do
> Sometimes, and yet shall like it too;
> Nor any notice take at all
> Of what, we gone, she would extol.
> (43, 29 - 40)

It reads curiously like a work of etiquette and is, in essence, a prescription for female *sprezzatura*, a guide to urbane behavior for the court lady, the game of courtly love defined. Finally the whole business bored Suckling and he preferred to laugh at it. But his laughter conforms to the description of behavior just quoted. That is, he creates a world of nuances, of ambiguities, of shifts and shades of meaning, of civilized subtleties and distances. At its best his poetry on love conforms to the fashions he prescribes.

"To a Lady that forbidd to love before Company" provides yet another example of Suckling's ability to shift tones and to play with and against poetic conventions. The opening is direct, dramatic, and one of those passages which points to Suckling's allegiance to Donne:

> What noe more favours, not A Ribbon more,
> Noe fanne, nor muffe to hold as heretofore?
>   (43, 1 - 2)

The lines are at once both dramatic and evocative of the whole world of the etiquette of fashionable love games. "Deare must I love you, yet not love you too?" (43, 10), the argument begins, after a list of the forms of courtship the lady has denied. The line has a neat balance, and the play on the two loves effectively locates the problem. The direct address reinforces the intensity and drama of the poem, a drama made ironic because the lady is denying what are, after all, Platonic poses:

> May we not looke our selves into a Traunce,
> Let our soules parly at our eyes, not glaunce,
> Not touch the hand, nor by soft wringing there
> Whisper a love that none but eyes can heare?
>   (43, 5 - 8)

The argument is delicate. The lady is too particular, too "nice." Observers can more easily detect the paths of birds or trace the line of stars than they can the course of love:

> Love is all spirit, fayries sooner may
> Bee taken Tardy when they night-tricks play
> Than wee; we are too safe I feare, that rather
> Would they could finde us both in bedd together!
>   (44, 17 - 20)

All the Platonic nuances, the fine and courtly argument, disappear in the comic reversal of the last line. The mockery of the Platonic conventions is so effective because Suckling handles them so easily and keeps such a straight face in the first nineteen lines.

II   *Melancholy Libertine*

The three poems called "Sonnet" I, II, and III are Suckling at his very best. They are, of course, not sonnets in the sense of fourteen lines of rhymed iambic pentameter but in the sense of short lyric pieces. Musical settings exist for both "Sonnet I" and "Sonnet II". Although "Sonnet III" most clearly belongs to the tradition of the love problem or love riddle, all three wittily explore the reality of traditional attitudes in love poetry.

"Sonnet I" is a kind of libertine's lament.

> Do'st see how unregarded now
>   that piece of beauty passes?
> There was a time when I did vow
>   to that alone;
>   but mark the fate of faces:
> That red and white works now no more on me
> Then if it could not charm or I not see.
> (47, 1 - 7)

The poem proposes a love riddle. How is it that the speaker can no longer love her when ". . . the face continues good, / and I have still desires" (8 - 9) and pleads for an answer:

> Oh! some kind power unriddle where it lies,
> Whether my heart be faulty, or her eyes?
> (13 - 14)

The third stanza restates the dilemma. Both he and she are still players in the game of love; both love and are loved, but no longer one another. The answer to the riddle, despite an almost elegiac note, is just to repeat the problem:

> Sure Beauties Empires, like to greater States
> Have certain periods set, and hidden fates.
> (48, 20 - 21)

So the poem asks why is it that one becomes bored with one beauty and seeks another, why must love be inconstant, and answers because that's the way it is. Both the speaker and the lady are trapped in an unending cycle of attraction - indifference - new attraction. It is a cycle that could be broken by a moralist, but the speaker is not a moralist. The poem sits on the edge of despair, but never admits it. Instead it achieves a gaiety tinged with an ironic melancholy because it accepts without question the inconstancy of love, the inevitability of bored satiety, and a return to the hunt in the search of novelty. Moreover, both the *he* and the *she* are caught in the same round; both are players in the same libertine game. But the melancholy, the potential despair, is all by implication, all subliminal. What one hears is a wry acceptance:

> but mark the fate of faces:
> That red and white works no more on me
> Then if it could not charm or I not see.
> (47, 5 - 7)

But the tone contains another nuance. The lady, fellow libertine or not, is "that piece of beauty"; indifference is the lot of "faces"; beauty is a matter of "red and white." The diction contains its own reductive ironies.

"Sonnet II" is less delicately maneuvered, more bluntly cynical. It too deals with sexual attraction but sees it in completely naturalistic terms. The poem is almost a politer version of "The deformed Mistress," for it denies in the first stanza the gentle art of flirtatious love play described in "To His Rival II"; the poem rejects the very existence of beauty in the second stanza and settles finally in the third for the reduction of all theories of love to appetite:

> 'Tis not the meat, but 'tis the appetite
> makes eating a delight
> and if I like one dish
> More than another, that a Pheasant is;
> What in our watches, that in us is found,
> So to the height and nick
> We up be wound,
> No matter by what hand or trick.
> (48, 49; 17 - 24)

Donne's "Communitie" is hardly any more brutal, "Chang'd loves are but chang'd sorts of meat."[3] "Sonnet II" is a libertine poem belonging to a tradition which includes writers as distant as Ovid and Montaigne.[4] The cynicism of the third stanza and the veritable lewdness of the *double entendres* of the last four lines are undeniable. Yet the brutality of the poem is moderated by the light touch, grace, and music of the lines:

> Of thee (kind boy) I ask no red and white
> to make up my delight,
> no odd becoming graces,
> Black eyes, or little know-not-whats, in faces.
> (48, 1 - 4)

The opening is disarmingly graceful. The invocation of Cupid, the black eyes, and the French "little know-not-whats" (in Letter No. 48, "certaine *je ne scay quoys*") establish a light, easy tone. The tone is sustained and works contrapuntally to the overt statement. Whatever darkness the poem contains is masked by the easy manner. Moreover, it must be recalled that the poem is a song with all the consequences of its musical setting. Finally the poem must be seen as much gesture and pose as "meaning."

"Sonnet III" takes another given of conventional love poetry, the idea that a faithful but losing lover will be united with the beloved after death, and mocks it. The first stanza, which sets up this love riddle:

> Oh! for some honest Lovers ghost,
>   Some kind unbodied post
>   Sent from the shades below.
>   I strangely long to know
> Whether the nobler Chaplets wear,
> Those that their mistresse scorn did bear,
>   Or those that were us'd kindly.
>   (49, 1 - 7)

is directly derived from John Donne's "Loves Deitie," which begins:

> I long to talke with some old lovers ghost,
>   Who dyed before the god of Love was borne:
> I cannot thinke that hee, who then lov'd most,
>   Sunke so low, as to love one which did scorne.[5]

But Suckling derived more than the opening from Donne, and "Sonnet III" can be seen as a variation upon and extension of a major idea in "Loves Deitie." "It cannot be Love, till I love her that loves mee," Donne asserts, and he goes on to declare that if we could free ourselves from the tyranny of love, we would never love where we weren't loved in return. Suckling is more direct, but the idea is the same:

> T'have lov'd alone will not suffice,
> Unlesse we also have been wise,
>   And have our Loves enjoy'd.
>   (49, 12 - 14)

How, he asks in the third stanza,

> . . . can that *Elizium* be
> Where I my Mistresse still must see
>   Circled in others Armes?
>   (19 - 21)

Love's martyrs may be awarded wreaths of bay or myrtle in heaven, but if that is all, he concludes, "Give me the Woman here" (50, 35).

The poem argues for physical love by deflating a romantic poetic tradition of forlorn lovers. Again Suckling achieves the major effect by the contrast of the lightness of tone with the direct bluntness of the concluding statement. He plays the absoluteness of his antiromanticism against the lilt of the verse and the invocation of the romantic tradition:

> For there the Judges all are just,
>   And *Sophonisba* must
>   Be his whom she held dear;
>   Not his who lov'd her here:
> The sweet *Philoclea* since she dy'de
> Lies by her *Pirocles* his side,
>   Not by *Amphialus*.
>   (49 - 50, 22 - 28)

Sophonisba, daughter of Hasdrubal, was forced to marry Syphax and later took poison; her sad tale provided grist for the dramatic mills. Philoclea, Pirocles, and Amphialus all belong to Sir Philip Sidney's romance *Arcadia*. The romantic figures of ballad tradition might have done as well, but the mockery is more directly aimed at courtly romanticism.

The three "Sonnets" all share in a rejection and mockery of the conventions of idealized love poetry and in particular of courtly-love poetry. Whatever disillusion may lurk below the surfaces and no matter how blunt and reductive the totality of the poems may be, they equally share the lightness, grace, and urbanity that is Suckling's special achievement.

III   *The Weary Lover*

That same lightness and urbanity characterize poems like "Loves Feast" ("I pray thee spare me, gentle Boy"), "The careless Lover," and "Womans Constancy" ("There never yet was woman made"), which express a general weary reaction to the whole matter of love. The speaker in "Loves Feast" is emotionally exhausted by love. His prayer to Cupid is to be let alone:

> I pray thee spare me, gentle Boy,
> Presse me no more for that slight toy,

> That foolish trifle of an heart;
> I swear it will not do its part,
> Though thou dost thine, employ'st thy power and art.
> (51, 1 - 5)

Even if the heart is only a slight toy (a favorite epithet for Suckling), it is worn out and has become

> Sullen and wise, will have its will,
> And like old Hawks pursues that still
> That makes least sport, flies onely where't can kill.
> (8 - 10)

Suckling uses images from hawking frequently; and the image here aptly reflects the attitude of the exhausted lover, a predatory lover, his energy sapped in the service of an insatiable god, that ironically "gentle Boy." The weary lover wants to be freed from any pretense that love is anything more than a brief appetite. He is too weary even for the libertine antifruition argument; instead of abstaining for any reason, even pleasure, he asserts:

> I shall be carving of the best,
> Rudely call for the last course 'fore the rest.
> (52, 14 - 15)

The emotions of love and its rituals can't be borne, but reducing it to the merely physical still yields no final satisfaction:

> And oh! when once that course is past,
> How short a time the Feast doth last!
> Men rise away, and scarce say grace,
> Or civilly once thank the face
> That did invite, but seek another place.
> (16 - 20)

There is nothing left. The possibilities of the Petrarchan, of the Platonic, of the naturalistic libertine are all exhausted.

What remains is style. The speaker has arrived at a perfectly untenable position at least within the context of the traditions of amorous verse. The rakehell persona of the poem sees and admits the futility of lust. Dante put it differently when he described the Lustful in the Second Circle of Hell:

> Like as the starlings wheel in the wintry season
>   In wide and clustering flocks wing-borne, wind-borne
>   Even so they go, the souls who did this treason,
> Hither and thither, and up and down, outworn,
> Hopeless of any rest—rest, did I say?
> Of the least minishing of their pangs forlorn.[6]

The juxtaposition of Suckling and Dante may appear capricious, but the justification lies in their shared perception of the nature of lust. Sir John is not taking the matter seriously, but his amusement in no way lessens the psychological perception. Still he avoids the consequences of the perception through the cheerful, graceful, undaunted manner of saying it. With the form and language of the love lyric he admits the futility of love. Congreve has Millamant quote this lyric in *The Way of the World* not because its overt statement is appropriate to a girl about to marry for love, but because its worldly, detached, wry style is appropriate to a vision of civilization.

"The Constant Lover" is a simpler poem. The speaker is a straightforward and unrepentant libertine:

> Out upon it, I have lov'd
>   Three whole days together;
> And am like to love three more,
>   If it hold fair weather.
>   (55, 1 - 4)

There is admittedly no weariness in this poem, probably Suckling's best known, rather an undaunted audacity, an explosive bounciness, and not a hint of repentance:

> Had it any been but she
>   And that very very Face,
> There had been at least ere this
>   A dozen dozen in her place.
>   (56, 13 - 16)

"The Answer" to it is linked with the name of the courtier and favorite of the queen, Sir Toby Mathew, but is almost certainly by Suckling.[7] The two poems together form a unit which allows for a coterie joke at the expense of Sir Toby as well as comically one-uping the libertine boast of "The Constant Lover." He, "The Answer" asserts, is a fool to have been faithful for three days:

> She to whom you were so true,
>   And that very very Face,
> Puts each minute such as you
>   A dozen dozen to disgrace.
>   (57, 13 - 16)

The female, "The Answer" declares, will out-libertine the male.
Together the pair make a comic negative. The gay and proud boast
of the happy libertine in "The Constant Lover" is a mockery; for all
his braggadocio, he's just a cuckold. The two poems create a dialectic which arrives once more at the negation of the possibilities of
poetic love conventions.

"The careless Lover," on the other hand, offers at least the
retreat of indifference. The pose is of the lighthearted, unattached,
unmoved lover:

> She's fair, she's wondrous fair,
> But I care not who know it,
> Ere I'le die for love, I'le fairly forgo it.
>   (57, 5 - 7)

So runs the refrain, with its first line suitable for a love song and the
last two refuting the song and the world of love. The careless lover
is totally free from the demands of conventional lovers for appropriate lovesick behavior. His heart is unattached and unaffected:

> *Black-Friars* to me, and old *Whitehall*,
> Is even as much as is the fall
> Of fountains or a pathless grove,
> And nourishes as much my love.
>   (58, 29 - 32)

His answer to the lovesickness of the conventions of love is the city
and society. Romantic pastoral settings leave the man of the city
cold:

> I visit, talk, do business, play,
> And for a need laugh out a day:
> Who does not thus in *Cupids* school,
> He makes not Love, but plays the Fool.
>   (58 - 59, 36 - 39)

Against the follies of love, the modish games and poses of courtly
romance, he offers heart-free indifference and the tough-minded
values of city life and society.

IV   *The Devil Take It*

All this may seem to imply a more specific progression or development in Suckling's poetry than is intended. The dating of the poems
is not absolutely certain; a chronological ordering is necessarily
sometimes approximate. Rather than as a chronological development of the rejection of conventional love themes, it is more accurate to see that rejection as the major and most successful poetic
theme among alternatives. One of the most successful and popular
of those rejections is the "Song" ("Why so pale and wan fond
Lover?"). It first appeared in *Aglaura* (IV, ii, 14 - 28), where Orsames sings it to the platonic ladies Semanthe and Orithie. L. A.
Beaurline finds the poem a prime example of Suckling's *elegant
facetiousness* and emphasizes the dramatic context and the resulting
"double audience" of the poem: "Suckling intends his song to be
overheard by the platonic ladies. Thus Orsames' song is not only advice to a fond lover but a pose of the gallant and a threat to any coy
mistress—if she does not return a man's love, if she does not react as
a flesh-and-blood human being, she will be left behind. . . . The
doubleness of the rhetorical situation is one of the reasons why this
poem is so charming and playful. It gives us, the general readers or
third audience, a special detachment. . . ."[8]
     The dramatic context of *Aglaura*, however, will be recalled by
only a few readers. For most readers the drama of the poem is only
that created by itself, without a specific situational context apart
from the literary conventions of the seventeenth century. Still, even
if the audience is reduced to the "fond lover" and ourselves, the
poem remains dramatic. The speaker is again the experienced older
lover, the world-weary and love-weary libertine. The poem is short
enough to quote in its totality.

> Why so pale and wan fond Lover?
>   Prithee why so pale?
> Will, when looking well can't move her,
>   Looking ill prevaile?
>   Prithee why so pale?

2.

Why so dull and mute young Sinner?
  Prithee why so mute?
Will, when speaking well can't win her,
  Saying nothing doo't?
  Prithee why so mute?

3.

Quit, quit, for shame, this will not move,
  This cannot take her;
If of her selfe she will not Love,
  Nothing can make her,
  The Devill take her.

(64)

The familiar pun on "fond" is repeated. In the second stanza the shift to "young Sinner" underlines the speaker's ironic approach to the lover, who is so clearly (and sadly) not a "sinner" at all; the jocular familiarity of the address is wittily edged.

The fond lover, moreover, is reduced to the barest minimum of description. He is "pale and wan" and "dull and mute." In brief, he is and acts the Petrarchan lover. The lady is unmoved by the poses of the wan and silent lover because she is the Petrachan mistress and by definition can't be moved; she is all ice. "If of her selfe she will not Love," but she cannot love of herself because she has no self, only her conventional being.

The situation suggests Pirandello. The two characters of the poem can only behave within the confines of the Petrarchan love conventions. The only way out of the dilemma is to destroy the convention. The poem is, then, Suckling's comic poetic curse of Petrarchanism and court Platonism. "The Devill take her" means more than just the icy lady; it means the whole set of literary and social poses. The sexual pun in "take" brightens the curse when the lady is seen not simply as the Petrarchan mistress but as the whole array of artifice in amorous verse.

Apart from the wit of the drama which expands the fiction to imply a larger literary and social critique, a large part of the poem's effectiveness comes from its guise of inevitability, its crisp, formulaic structure. The syllogism looks so solid. The first two stanzas are identical questions, one asking about appearances, the other about speech. The comic and incongruous rhymes, *Lover, move her; prevaile, pale* of the first stanza are matched by those of the second, *Sinner, win her; doo't, mute.* The third stanza achieves its conclusive terminal quality by variations in stress and the repetitive *hers.* The song is a triumph of economy of language and effective repetition, of the appearance of simplicity and ease.

If "Why so pale and wan fond Lover?" can be viewed as a dismissal of an array of poetic conventions, "Farewel to Love" expands the dismissal to the whole experience of love. It is a curious and interesting poem of a sort one would not have expected Suckling to have written. The poem shows the influence of Donne's "Farewel to Love" and "Ecclogue 1613"; to the latter in some lines, to the former in general theme. Suckling's "Farewel to Love," however, appears, at least at first reading, more serious than Donne's and recalls the whole tradition of medieval rejections of love.

> But my dear nothings, take your leave,
> No longer must you me deceive,
>   (66, 6 - 7)

seems light and airy enough, but by the sixth stanza the speaker has achieved the dark vision of mortality Eliot describes in "Whispers of Immortality":

> Webster was much possessed by death
> And saw the skull beneath the skin;
> And breastless creatures under ground
> Leaned backward with a lipless grin.[9]

Suckling and Webster are odd bedfellows, but the perceptions are the same:

> If I gaze now, 'tis but to see
> What manner of deaths-head 'twill be,
>   When it is free
> From that fresh upper skin,
> The gazers Joy, and sin.
>   (67, 26 - 30)

The problem, however, is that the tone is so dubious:

> The Locks, that curl'd o're each eare be,
> Hang like two Master-worms to me,

> That (as we see)
> Have tasted to the rest
> Two holes, where they lik't best.

9·

> A quick corse me-thinks I spy
> In ev'ry woman; . . . .

10·

> They mortifie, not heighten me
> These of my sins the Glasses be:
>   And here I see
> How I have lov'd before.
> *And so I love no more.*
>   (41 - 42, 46 - 50)

The sentiments are certainly properly pious. The poem, set at the end of the poems in *Fragmenta Aurea*, offers a traditional Christian retraction to the worldly verse. The difficulty is believing that Sir John is not spoofing such conventional pieties and having a marvelous time teasing the Amaranthas, Lucindas, Celias, and Aglauras of court poetry by these gruesome emblems of mortality. The grisly and solemn religious mask might be one he would enjoy donning. He certainly was not a man for pieties himself. Serious or not, however, "Farewel to Love" does mark a farewell to love poetry, for the poems of the last years are centrally social in theme and manner.

Suckling's "love" poetry, then, is primarily a rejection of the whole tradition. A. J. Smith observes cogently that Suckling "saw as clearly as Rochester what fashionable life now offered. His poetry offers our earliest example of a life centered in a style, which in his case draws out a lively but in the end desperately skeptical view of sexual life as a focus of life altogether."[10]

Indeed, it is not a long step from Suckling to Rochester; a parallel in terms of style in the graphic arts can be found in the series of etchings, *Miseries of War*, by Suckling's older French contemporary Jacques Callot. Callot depicts the savagery of war literally, but depicts it with a consummately elegant line. The feet of soldiers in the execution squad are turned gracefully as they might be in a dance step, but their gavotte is mortal. Style and content play ironically against one another. This is Suckling's achievement in his poetry of love. His final comment on the whole tradition is a dismissive "the Devil take it, " but the dismissal is elegant, amused, and civilized.

CHAPTER 7

Poems: The Social Voice
(1637 - 1641)

I   The Club

T HE last four years of Suckling's life include the writing
of *Aglaura, An Account of Religion by Reason, The Goblins,*
Brennoralt, and nine poems, including "The Wits," "A Ballade
Upon a Wedding," and "Upon my Lord Brohalls Wedding." These
years also include the raising of his hundred horse for the First
Bishops' War, appointment as a Gentleman of the Privy Chamber,
election to Parliament, participation in the Second Bishops' War,
involvement in the Army Plot, and his final exile. In short they were
years of activity not only in literary matters but in the world of
political and military affairs as well. *Aglaura, An Account of*
Religion by Reason, and "The Wits" were all apparently written in
1637. They represent a wide range of interests. The latter two in
particular show Suckling reaching out beyond the court to less cir-
cumscribed concerns and audience; both indicate, moreover, a
wider group of acquaintances. In 1638 Wye Saltonstall dedicated
his *Ovid de Ponto* to Suckling and Thomas Nabbes did the same
with his play *Covent Garden.* These dedications, as well as Lord
Dudley North's letter to Suckling, accompanying a copy of
"Concerning Petty Poetry," indicate Suckling's growing reputation
as a man of letters.

The poems belonging to these years are primarily social and
literary in nature. Two poems are occasioned by weddings, but both
of them focus more sharply on the social than the amatory aspects.
With the exception of "Upon my Lord Brohalls Wedding" the
poems of these years abandon the rakehell themes and tone and
adopt a different voice, a voice that is essentially urbane, urban, and
social.

135

"A Summons to Town" is Suckling's only verse epistle, but even
the single appearance of the genre marks the wider and more social
turn in his poetry. "A Summons to Town" is apparently addressed
to John Hales, a distinguished scholar and theologian, fellow of
Eton College and one of the group associated with Lucius Cary,
Lord Falkland, and his intellectual circle at Great-Tew. Edward
Hyde, Earl of Clarendon, Suckling's contemporary who was to
become Lord Chancellor of England, says of Hales:

Being a Person of the greatest Eminency for Learning, and other Abilities,
from which He might have promised any Preferment in the Church, He
withdrew himself from all Pursuits of that Kind, into a private Fellowship
in the College of *Eton* . . . where He lived amongst his Books, and the
most separated from the World of any Man then living; though He was not
in the least Degree inclined to Melancholy, but on the contrary, of a very
open and pleasant Conversation; and therefore was very well pleased with
the Resort of his Friends to him, who were such as He had chosen, and in
whose Company He delighted, and for whose Sake He would sometimes,
once a Year, resort to *London*, only to enjoy their chearful Conversation.[1]

Sir John Suckling was one of those London friends. "A Summons to
Town" urges Hales to leave his theological studies and "straight
bestride the Colledge Steed" (70, 8) to come to London and its
pleasures:

> The sweat of learned *Johnsons* brain,
> And gentle *Shakespear's* eas'er strain,
> A hackney-couch conveys you to,
> In spite of all that rain can do:
> And for your eighteen pence you sit
> The Lord and Judge of all fresh wit.
> (21 - 26)

"A Summons" reverses the more familiar pattern of the Horatian
appeal to retreat from the city to the country found in such a poem
as Carew's "To my friend G. N. from Wrest." The theater, good
food, wine, dry transportation, and the pleasures of witty conversation are the urban lures Suckling offers Hales.

As is appropriate for a verse epistle "A Summons" is simple and
informal in style. Suckling jokes lightly about Hales's theological
studies:

> Leave *Socinus* and the Schoolmen,
> (Which *Jack Bond* swears do but fool men)
>   (9 - 10)

but the joke is part of an overall compliment to Hales. Further, it
reminds the reader of Suckling's own claim of admission to the intellectual community, *An Account of Religion By Reason.* The compliment to Hales is casual and easy, without the slightest hint of
flattery. The poem moves on to develop a cheerful, jocular irony in
a hyperbolic vision of the social world of London where one can
meet

> . . . . . . men so refin'd,
> Their very common talk at boord,
> Makes wise, or mad a young Court-Lord,
> . . . .
> Where no disputes nor forc't defence
> Of a mans person for his sence
> Take up the time, all strive to be
> Masters of truth, as victory:
> And where you come, I'de boldly swear
> A Synod might as eas'ly erre.
>   (71, 32 - 42)

The ironical twitting is capped by the reference to the Synod in
the last line, for Hales attended the Synod of Dort (1618 - 1619) as
chaplain to Sir Dudley Carleton, the English ambassador to the
Netherlands: "and hath left the best Memorial behind him, of the
Ignorance, and Passion, and Animosity, and Injustice of that
Convention; of which He often made very pleasant Relations;
though at that Time it received too much Countenance from
England."[2]
The line manages to compliment Hales by reference to his experience, to a subject of his conversation. Clarendon's description of
Hales's references to Dort as "very pleasant Relations," moreover,
suggests that Hales spoke of the Synod of Dort in a humorous and
ironic fashion, spoke, in short, with a tone much like that Suckling
adopts in "A Summons to Town." The compliment to Hales is obvious enough, but the easy, ironic wit so qualifies it, makes it so
clearly friendly that its modest and retiring recipient could receive
the poem in a perfectly comfortable manner.

"He loved Canarie [wine]; but moderately, to refresh his spirits,"
John Aubrey tells us of Hales, whom he personally visited, finding
him "a prettie little man, sanguine, of a cheerful countenance, very
gentile, and courteous. . . ."[3] Hales was anything but a rakehell
courtier. His natural milieu was the cloistered shelter of Eton. His
delights were books and conversation. Given a description of this
sort, one might not expect to find Suckling writing him this sociable
appeal. The fact that he does marks a major shift in Suckling's
poetry. That the appeal is to come to the city underlines the nature
of the shift. City versus country is one of the major themes of the
Restoration, and Suckling's poem is a precursor of that theme as it is
of the movement toward public, social poetry in the latter half of
the seventeenth century.

II   "The Wits"

The shift to social poetry is seen strikingly in his major poem of
this period, "The Wits" or "A Sessions of the Poets." The poem is
called "A Sessions of the Poets" in *Fragmenta Aurea*, but "The
Wits" is a more appropriate title not only because of manuscript
authority and contemporary references, but also because that title
more accurately describes the participants in the "sessions."

> A Sessions was held the other day,
> And *Apollo* himself was at it (they say;)
> The Laurel that had been so long reserv'd,
> Was now to be given to him best deserv'd.
>   (71, 1 - 4)

The sessions is held so that Apollo may award the laureate bays,[4]
but not all those present could be serious contenders. Many of the
participants are gentlemanly poetasters at best. The gathering is
clearly more correctly seen as a society of wits than of poets. If we
find poets of note—Ben Jonson, William Davenant, Thomas Carew,
Thomas May, George Sandys, and Edmund Waller, we also find
scholars—John Hales of Eton, John Selden, William Chillingworth;
and courtiers who at the most wrote poems incidentally as a
gentleman ought—William Murray, for example, a Gentleman of
the Bedchamber who later became the first Earl of Dysart and who
had, the *Dictionary of National Biography* records, "one particular
quality, that when he was drunk, which was very often, he was

upon a most exact reserve, though he was pretty open at other times."

"The Wits" is of considerable social interest, for it shows something of the complexity and range of the society in which Suckling moved. A thorough analysis of that aspect belongs to the social historian, but one can note that the wits of the poem are drawn from at least three overlapping, interlocking but still distinct groups. The largest is of courtiers; at least fifteen of the twenty-two wits have clear court associations. Most of these held court appointments, and most of them had strong associations with Queen Henrietta Maria and her court faction.

Another group is identified with Lucius Cary, Lord Falkland, and his circle of intellectual and scholarly friends; this group often overlaps still another society, that connected with the law and the Inns of Court. Twelve of the twenty-two are mentioned by Charles II's future Lord Chancellor and Earl of Clarendon, Edward Hyde, in his *Life*, as friends during his days as a law student or later: Thomas Carew, Lucius Cary, William Chillingworth, Sir Kenelm Digby, Sidney Godolphin, John Hales, Ben Jonson, Thomas May, John Selden, Sir John Vaughan, Edmund Waller, and Sir Francis Wenman. Hyde doesn't mention his former roommate at the Middle Temple, the scapegrace William Davenant, [5] but in the *Life* the earl looks back on his wild youth with considerable distaste: ". . . there never was an Age, in which in so short a Time, so many young Gentlemen, who had not Experience in the World, or some tutelar Angel to protect them, were insensibly and suddenly overwhelmed in that Sea of Wine, and Women, and Quarrels, and Gaming, which almost overspread the whole Kingdom, and the Nobility and Gentry thereof."[6] It is not surprising that Hyde fails to mention his own exact contemporary, Davenant's good friend, Sir John Suckling, who was only too willing to sail on that sea of wine, women, quarrels and gaming; nor is it, contrariwise, surprising that Suckling omits Hyde, for all their mutual friends, from the convivial gathering of "The Wits."

If the poem was the "Ballad made of the Wits sung to the King when he was in *New Forest*"[7] in the late summer of 1637, the social nature of the poem is even more manifest. The poem uses an ostensible literary occasion, the sessions itself, Apollo's awarding of the laureate bays, to celebrate a society. The kind of social links seen in "The Wits" and something of the atmosphere of literary debate are found in the traditional story of the argument between Suckling and Ben Jonson which Nicholas Rowe recounted in his edition of Shakespeare: "In a Conversation between Sir *John Suckling*, Sir *William D'Avenant, Endymion Porter*, Mr. *Hales* of Eaton, and *Ben Johnson*, Sir *John Suckling*, who was a profess'd admirer of *Shakespear*, had undertaken his Defence against *Ben Johnson* with some warmth; Mr. *Hales*, who had sat still for some time, hearing *Ben* frequently reproaching him with the want of Learning, and Ignorance of the Antients, told him at last, 'That if Mr. *Shakespeare* had not read the Antients, he had likewise not stollen any thing from 'em'; (a fault the other made no Conscience of)."[8] Jonson receives rough treatment from Suckling in "The Wits." He is twitted for publishing his folio *Workes of Benjamin Jonson:*

> . . . he told them plainly he deserv'd the Bayes,
> For his were call'd Works, where others were but Plaies;
> (72, 19 - 20)

but the joke was a familiar one, for Jonson's audacity in the matter was a major subject for gossip and witticisms at the time, and Jonson does at least receive two stanzas to himself, and compliments along with taunts.

"The Wits" is admittedly important as a fictional-narrative work of literary criticism.[9] Carew is criticized for his "hard bound" Muse, for poems

> . . . brought forth but with trouble and pain.
>   And
> All that were present there did agree,
> A Laureats Muse should be easie and free.
> (73, 35 - 38)

Walter Montague is teased for the unintelligibility and, by implication, the Platonic preciousness of his wordy pastoral play, *The Shepheard's Paradise*, in which Queen Henrietta Maria and her maids of honor acted before the king in 1632. Sir William Berkeley is assured that all mean well toward him but will reserve their critical judgment until "they . . . see how his snow would sell" (73, 50), which may be a reference to the manner and content of his play, *The Lost Lady*.[10] The diminutive courtier and Member of Parliament Sidney Godolphin is advised "not to write so strong" (75, 92), to avoid, in other words, those "strong lines" in the manner of Donne which critics such as Dudley, Lord North, deplored. The general critical stance of the poem is for poetry that is natural and open, "easie and free."

Literary criticism, however, is always in passing and subordinate to the poem's social intent. It, like "A Summons to Town," is a clubby poem; its pleasures are greatest for the members of the club. The pleasures are those of inclusion and of sharing mutual likes and dislikes. Familiar companionable jokes are repeated; the club members are teased in the poem as they are over their wine. Jonson's presumed pretentiousness in publishing his *Works;* Davenant's unfortunate lack of a nose; Suckling's own insouciant attitude toward poetry and his preference for "black eyes" or a "lucky hit / At bowls" (74, 77 - 78) all receive comment. The gossipy and bustling Toby Mathew, always whispering in someone's ear, is admitted only because of his "Character" (a brief essay) of Lady Carlisle:

> For
> Had not her Character furnisht you out
> With something of handsome, without all doubt
> You and your sorry Lady Muse had been
> In the number of those that were not to come in.
> (74, 61 - 64)

The final awarding of the laurel to an alderman underlines the courtly quality of the poem, with its aristocratic gibe at the city and city money. Finally, the fullest compliment in the poem is given to Lucius Cary, Lord Falkland:

> He was of late so gone with Divinity,
> That he had almost forgot his Poetry,
> Though to say the truth (the *Apollo* did know it)
> He might have been both his Priest and his Poet.
> (75, 99 - 102)

And Falkland, the Sidney of his age, undoubtedly was the man most admired by all the groups bound into the social world of "The Wits."

"The Wits" belongs to the ballad tradition,[11] its ballad story a social narrative. The stanzaic form is suitable for the narrative and for the jocular tone of the poem, being a variation of the old bob and wheel, each stanza consisting of two quatrains joined by a one-word "bob."[12] Michael Drayton's "The Sacrifice to Apollo" surely had no direct influence on "The Wits," but its links with the "Tribe of Ben" and their meetings in the "Apollo Room" of the Devil Tavern suggest again the social and clubby background of the poem. Certainly somewhere in the inspirational vicinity of "The Wits" are Jonson's own verses "Over the Door at the Entrance into the Apollo":

> Welcome all that lead or follow,
> To the Oracle of Apollo—
> Here he speaks out of his Pottle,
> Or the Tripos, his Tower Bottle:
> All his answers are Divine,
> Truth it self doth flow in wine.[13]

Another poem possibly connected with "The Wits" is "On the Time-Poets"; as Clayton points out, it is an extract from William Heminge's *Elegy on Randolph's Finger*, c. 1630 - 32. It opens with a reference to Apollo:

> One night the great Apollo pleas'd with *Ben*,
> Made the odde number of the Muses ten;[14]

and is a kind of catalogue of poets with a comment for each. Suckling, it has been seen, was not so pleased with Ben and might have written "The Wits" partly in reaction to it.[15]

But finally "The Wits" is also an original poem which sets rather than follows a fashion. Professor Clayton cites Samuel Johnson's recognition of "The Wits" in the *Lives of the English Poets* as "'a mode of satire . . . first introduced by Suckling'" and notes the "many . . . imitations, including, for example, poems by (or attributed to) John Wilmot, Earl of Rochester; John Sheffield, first Duke of Buckingham and Normandy; Leigh Hunt; and James Russell Lowell; as well as . . . anonymous poems."[16] Satire that it is at times, "The Wits" is basically a complimentary social poem. Its brief moments of literary criticism are themselves social, that is, expressions of the values and standards of the group saluted in the poem. It is, more specifically, a court poem; most of its participants are courtiers, and if it was sung before the king in New Forest, its courtliness is even more evident. To the world of the court and to the court poem, however, Suckling adds the intellectual, literary worlds of London taverns and the Inns of Court and of learned country gentlemen,—Falkland, Wenman, and their university friends. In short, Suckling modifies the court poem into the club poem and develops a social voice of the sort which will dominate the poetry of the coming age. Apart from its social and critical interest "The Wits" is a lively and sprightly work showing Suckling at his "natural and easy" best.

III   *Two Wedding Poems*

If imitations and parodies are a measure of popularity, "A Ballade. Upon a Wedding" was one of Suckling's most popular poems, and it retains its popularity. Like "The Wits" it too establishes a poetic vogue, the parodistic, countrified epithalamium. The poem most probably celebrates the marriage of John, Lord Lovelace and Lady Anne, the fifteen year old daughter of Thomas Wentworth, first Earl of Cleveland.[17] The couple was married on July 11, 1638; their marriage was also poetically celebrated by Thomas Carew with "An Hymeneall Song on the Nuptials of the Lady *Ann Wentworth*, and the Lord *Lovelace*." Carew's poem is written in a verse pattern similar to Suckling's, but Carew's is a serious and traditional epithalamium:

> Their kisses measure as they flow,
> Minutes, and their embraces show
> The howers as they passe.[18]

Carew's poem is graceful and effective, but thoroughly familiar in style and approach. It contrasts sharply with the brilliance and originality of Suckling's "A Ballade."

The achievement of "A Ballade" is in accomplishing the aims of a tradition by mocking it. The speaker of "A Ballade" is presumably a rustic who is almost, but not quite, overwhelmed by the brilliance of the aristocratic wedding party observed at Charing Cross, close to where the farmers come to sell their hay:

> I tell thee *Dick*, where I have been,
> Where I the rarest things have seen,
> Oh things beyond compare!
> (79, 1 - 3)

His enthusiasm is unbounded; the country does not hold people like this. The bridegroom is handsomer than even

>   . . . lusty *Roger* . . .,
>   Or little *George* upon the Green,
>   Or *Vincent* of the Crown.
>   (80, 22 - 24)

But naturally the greatest praise is reserved for the bride. Her smallness and delicacy are stressed:

>   Her feet beneath her Petticoat,
>   Like little mice stole in and out,
>   As if they fear'd the light:
>   But oh! she dances such a way!
>   No Sun upon an Easter day
>   Is half so fine a sight.
>   (81, 43 - 48)

The suggestion of Robert Herrick's lines

>   Her pretty feet
>   Like snailes did creep
>   A little out, and then,
>   As if they started at Bo-peep,
>   Did soon draw in agen. [19]

is totally appropriate, and Suckling does out-Herrick Herrick here. There is a country freshness and innocence to "A Ballade," but both are qualified by a cheerful and wholesome bawdry and by the speaker's naive literalness.

The speaker is delighted with the bride's pretty little mouth and describes it with a charming image:

>   Her mouth so small when she doth speak
>   Thou'dst swear her teeth her words did break,
>   That they might passage get.
>   (61 - 63)

The figure might be Herrick's, but the stanza concludes with a deliberate literalism which asserts the naiveté of the speaker and reinforces the sophisticated comedy of "A Ballade":

>   But she so handles still the matter,
>   They come as good as ours, or better,
>   And are not spoil'd one whit.
>   (82, 64 - 66)

The speaker is not a poet, but a literal countryman. His poetry is only that of enthusiasm and of delight in the beauty of the bride. The dramatic device gives Suckling a way of complimenting the wedding party that is both novel and amusing.

Stanza 13, which concludes the first movement of the poem, in terms of Carew's poem, the progress "to the Temple, and the Priest," intensifies the comedy and the witty play of "A Ballade'" against the traditional epithalamium with cheerful bawdiness:

> If wishing should be any sin,
> The Parson self had guilty bin,
>   (she lookt that day so purely;)
> And did the youth so oft the feat
> At night, as some did in conceit,
>   It would have spoil'd him, surely.
>   (73 - 78)

The effect is to insure that the preceding compliments remain anything but mawkish. The impropriety is the salt of the joke. The relationship of the audience to the speaker and to the poet is complex. The audience is both praised and mocked; it is above the speaker's rusticity, but the speaker deflates any superiority by asserting their similarities.

The second section of the poem moves inevitably to the marriage feast and to the nuptial bed. The feast is described as that of a country wedding. The guests are seated before grace is said, "hatts fly off, and youths carrouse . . ." (83, 97). The aristocrats are transformed into peasants; and in the last stanza Lord Lovelace and his bride, after all the hyperbolic compliment, are restored to the ordinary world, to the common level of humanity:

> At length the candles out, and now
> All that they had not done, they do:
>   What that is, who can tell?
> But I beleeve it was no more
> Than thou and I have done before
>   With *Bridget*, and with *Nell*.
>   (84, 127 - 32)

Herbert Berry is undoubtedly correct when he says, "The 'Ballade' contains more lyrical rapture than anything else Suckling ever wrote."[20] However, the rapture is colored by the good-natured bawdry and comedy of the speaker; it is the rapture of high spirits, of sheer exuberance. Thomas Randolph, a contemporary of Suckling, also has a rustic speaker in "The milk-maids Epithalamium," but Randolph's poem is far more conventional; it does not attempt realistic country speech and is less comic. A comparison of Randolph's and Suckling's poems makes clear the importance of audience and speaker in "A Ballade." The primary audience of "A Ballade" is the wedding party. They are, as said before, both complimented and teased by the speaker. They are consciously superior to the fictional speaker and yet are reminded of their final equality with him. The poem works against the whole epithalamium tradition by removing the possibility of elegant idealization; coitus, Suckling reminds us, is a great leveler. Still another aspect affecting the poem's audience is the awareness of the author, of Sir John, manipulating his fictional speaker in order to tease and to shock. The secondary audience, the audience not in the wedding party and not directly teased, watches the whole scene as one might a court masque. "A Ballade" is, then, eminently a social poem. Any epithalamium is, of course, social; but the difference between Carew's "A Hymeneall Song" and Suckling's "A Ballade. Upon a Wedding" is not just that between conventional and unconventional, serious and witty, but a larger one of focus and intent. Carew's poem celebrates a wedding; Suckling's celebrates a society.

The last poem to be considered, "Upon my Lord Brohalls Wedding," was occasioned by the marriage of Roger Boyle, Baron Broghill, to Lady Margaret Howard on January 27, 1641. The poem is an epithalamium more by courtesy than fact. It is a dialogue between S. and B., Suckling and, to name the most likely candidates, either Jack Barry or Jack Bond.[21] Whatever the identity of B., his attitude toward marriage is jesting and cynical while S. takes a more conventional, positive position toward love and marriage:

> S.   In bed dull man?
> When *Love* and *Hymens* Revels are begun,
> And the Church Ceremonies past and done?
> B.   Why who's gone mad to day?
>
> (86, 1 - 4)

But the point of the poem is not really to debate the question of marriage versus libertine freedom or actually to celebrate the wedding of Lord Broghill and Lady Margaret. Rather the poem exists to play wittily on the past circumstances of Broghill's romantic life. It is a piece of gossip turned to social verse.

Less than a year before his marriage Broghill had been engaged to Francis Harrison, one of the queen's maids of honor, and he had fought a duel over her.[22] The engagement obviously did not last, and Broghill's marriage to Lady Margaret Howard clearly was a bit of juicy and amusing gossip. A tactful epithalamium would hardly picture the bridegroom marrying "on the rebound," but "Upon my Lord Brohalls Wedding" goes out of its way to do so. Broghill is married with "A sprigg of Willow in his hat . . . / The loosers badge and liv'ry heretofore" (87, 17 - 18). S. and B. develop the theme until S. finally concludes wittily:

> But was the fair Nymphs praise or power lesse
> That led him captive now to happinesse,
> 'Cause she did not a forreign aid despise,
> But enterr'd breaches made by others eyes?
>   The Gods forbid!
> There must be some to shoot and batter down,
>   Others to force and to take in the Town.
>   To Hawkes (good *Jack*) and hearts
>   There may
>   Be sev'ral waies and Arts:
> One watches them perchance, and makes them tame;
> Another, when they're ready, shews them game.
>   (29 - 40)

The audience for this poem is certainly less the wedding party (obviously Lady Margaret could hardly have greeted such verse with much enthusiasm) than the larger social world of the court. The metaphors of siege and hawking belong to libertine poetry, and the attitudes of "Upon my Lord Brohalls Wedding" are libertine. The poem is of the sort that would be appropriate for the modern institution of the bachelor's dinner. The wedding is the occasion for the poem; the purpose of the poem is the social joke.

Amusing as it is, "Upon my Lord Brohalls Wedding" is darker and more cynical than either "The Wits" or "A Ballade. Upon a Wedding," but the times were darker. The latter two poems were written in a period of literary and social success for Suckling. They represent the high-water mark of his career. "Upon my Lord Brohalls Wedding" was written only a few months before Suckling's flight to France.

In these social poems, and in "The Wits" and "The Ballade" in particular, one can see the promise of a poetic future cut short by exile and early death. Such poetic maturity as Suckling finally found was outside the conventions and anticonventions of the love lyric. His bent is ultimately social; his public is still limited, but broadened far beyond the coterie world of the court to include the intellectual, literary world of the city, the Devil Tavern, the Inns of Court, and of the great houses of the learned gentry and nobility. These last poems of Suckling's look from the court to the coffeehouse; the society poet becomes the social poet. In this turning from the narrow and exhausted traditions of the courtly love lyric to the social poem Suckling is as forward-looking and "modern" as his friend Davenant with his introduction of the opera and stage innovations a decade later.

CHAPTER 8

"*Right Worthy of His Honours*": Reputation, Influences, and Achievement

I   *Reputation*

E PITAPHS are hardly an accurate measure of merit and reputation; exaggeration usually precedes oblivion.

> Thinke on a schollar without pride,
> A Souldier with much bloud un-dyed,
> A Statesman, yet noe whit ambitious,
> A Libertine, and yet not vitious
> Thinke to the heigth, if man could bee,
> Or ere was perfect, this was hee:
>
> Twas *Suckling*, hee who, though his ashes have,
> His honoured name shall never finde a grave.[1]

Perhaps the only parts of these lines concluding an epitaph attributed to James Paulin to which one could wholeheartedly subscribe are the assertions that Suckling died and his memory has not. Suckling's death was met with Royalist encomia such as this but also with taunts and mockery from the Puritan camp. His fame and his notoriety both owed a good deal to his early death as a putative Royalist martyr. The Hamletlike mixture of scholar, soldier, statesman need not be taken very seriously but indicates the heights to which Suckling's posthumous reputation could reach.

The status of his literary reputation within five years of his death is shown by the publication of *Fragmenta Aurea* in 1646. The popularity of this collection is evidenced by the publication of a second edition in 1648. The poetical tributes to Suckling found in the last half of the seventeenth century are not surprisingly most often highly exaggerated and of dubious worth as criticism or as a gauge of reputation. If Suckling was praised in high terms by a number of minor poets ("Sweet *Suckling* then, the glory of the Bower"[2]), the major writers of the period maintained a discreet silence.

After the restoration of Charles II Suckling's stock, as the epitome of the court wit of the old days and the exemplar, as Dryden saw him, of the gentlemanly style, rose sharply. In 1692 William Walsh found ". . . nothing more gay or sprightly than those [poems] of Sir John Suckling."[3] The comment is representative of a consistent theme in such criticism as exists—praise for Suckling's gaiety, his high spirits. Millamant's delight in "natural, easy Suckling" in *The Way of the World* establishes the extent to which Suckling represented a desired model of style and tone in the Restoration. By the middle of the eighteenth century taste had shifted, and Theophilus Cibber's hostility reflects an ear trained on regularity: "Sir John Suckling seems to have been no poet, nor to have had even the most distant appearances of it; his lines are generally so unmusical that none can read them without grating their ears; . . . as he is destitute of poetical conceptions, as well as the power of numbers, he has no pretensions to rank among the good poets."[4]

A century later David Masson made a far more friendly and favorable assessment: "For one who now reads anything of Carew there are twenty who know by heart some verses of his friend and brother-courtier, Sir John Suckling. His ballad upon a wedding, with the necessary omission of a verse or two, is in all the books of poetic extracts."[5] Another nineteenth-century commentator, after deploring, as one might expect in the age of Bowdler, the "unsightly and noisome weeds" among Suckling's flowers, concludes his comment with the by now traditional praise that "his imagination never awes, nor does his feeling stir us deeply; but his fancy pleases us, his wit and gaiety provoke a smile, and his careless ease and grace charm us."[6] At the start of the twentieth century Suckling's reputation was strong enough to merit A. H. Thompson's edition in 1910 and substantial praise in the *Cambridge History of English Literature:* "'Easy, natural Suckling' [sic] has won for himself, since the days of the restoration and Congreve's Millamant, an assured place in the bead-roll of English poets as the typical cavalier lyricist, the archrepresentative of Pope's 'mob of gentlemen who wrote with ease' lighthearted songs of courtly gallantry."[7] F. W. Moorman, the author of this commentary, does, however, credit Suckling with a serious side, noting the friendship with Hales and Falkland and the sober prose of the letter to Jermyn and *An Account of Religion by Reason.* George Saintsbury is equally positive. He links Suckling with Lovelace and finds Suckling distinctly superior: "True, he is often careless in the bad sense as well as in the good. . . . But in his own vein, that of coxcombry that is not quite cynical, and is quite intelligent, he is marvellously happy . . . we go to him for his easy grace, his agreeable impudence, his scandalous mock disloyalty . . . to the 'Lord of Terrible Aspect,' whom all his elder contemporaries worshipped so piously."[8]

Suckling's reputation has always been mixed and qualified. Typical of more recent assessments is that by Tucker Brooke:

Of all the "Cavalier" group Suckling had the most interesting mind and the largest potentialities for poetry. . . . But his potentialities were mainly unrealized. His four plays . . . are arid and ill-constructed, too full of melodramatic contrivance and undeveloped characters, and are written in the loosest of blank verse. Their only interest today is in the wealth of literary allusion they contain to Shakespeare and other earlier poets. . . . His best verses are the lightest. . . . Yet, though there was little faith in him and little warmth, Suckling usually has something to say. . . .[9]

The continued endurance of his reputation, however, is probably more accurately measured by the number of editions of his work than by the ups and downs of critical commentary. Since the publication of *Fragmenta Aurea* in 1646 an edition or reissue of his work has appeared at least every quarter century with the exception of the 1725 - 50 period. If one were to enumerate the inclusion of some of his poems in miscellanies and anthologies, his popular appeal would undoubtedly appear even greater. Suckling's place in English literature has never been large. He has always, and rightly so, been seen as a minor poet, but his position has always been secure; he has been continuously read. Nonacademic testimony for a minor poet of the seventeenth century is so rare that it cannot be ignored, particularly when felicitously phrased, as is Ogden Nash's tribute to Suckling in his poem "Brief Lives in Not so Brief II":

> I am fond of the late poet Sir John Suckling.
> He may have been no Swan of Avon, but he was a pretty
>   talented Twickenham Duckling.
> Along with a gift for poesy, he was possessed of ingenuity
>   and effrontery.[10]

II   *Schools and Influences*

Certainly another measure of Suckling's reputation is his influence on other poets. A part of that influence can be found in the
appendixes of the Oxford edition, which contain some of the
answers to and lampoons of Suckling's poems. Edmund Waller
answered "Against Fruition I" ("Stay here fond youth and ask no
more, be wise"), as did a far less distinguished poet, Henry Bold.
These and other answers, as well as lampoons like "Upon Sir John
Suckling's hundred horse" ("I tell thee *Jack* thou'st given the
King"), which mock Suckling in his own manner, all point to the
currency of his style. More notable, however, is the influence of
both "The Wits" and "A Ballade. Upon a Wedding." Both poems
were sufficiently popular and successful to establish minor genres.
If social change has made imitations of "A Ballade" impossible,
"The Wits" may have a distant modern descendant in the annual
New Year verse published in *The New Yorker.* Suckling's influence,
however, belongs to his own time and to the Restoration. His (yet
once again) naturalness and ease, his quintessential urbanity,
provided a model for a changing civilization which could no longer
look to the Petrarchan courtier for guidance. The specific and individual influence of particular poems, an influence in the main of
minor poems on minor poets, is far less important than the alter-
native of style and of manner that Suckling presented to his contemporaries and his immediate successors.
    Suckling founded no poetic school; "The Sucklington Faction" is
the title of an anti-Royalist tract and not a record of influence. Just
as it is impossible to establish a poetic Sucklington faction, it is
equally impossible to place Suckling himself unequivocally within
an established poetic school. The best one can do is to say that he
draws on the techniques and styles of both Jonson and Donne. His
clarity and directness he derives from Jonson; his irony, the main
thrust of his wit, his audaciousness, and his colloquial address he
takes from Donne. But the "hard lines" and the "metaphysical"
conceits of Donne and the learned labor and classical precision of
Jonson he rejects. He is the avowed amateur, the gentleman for
whom verse must give way to "black eyes, or a lucky hit / At
bowls. . . ." The care devoted to his poetry is to achieve that
artlessness, that *sprezzatura* prized by the age and clearly described
by Lord Dudley North in "Concerning petty Poetry": ". . . wit
needs not a rich stuffe; and art is best exprest where it least

appeares."[11] Suckling belongs finally to no one school because, at least in the poetry, his art is so often an adversary art. His relation to tradition and to current convention is most often mocking and ironic. His urbanity requires distance.

Suckling is, poetically, his own man, but in his independence he comes closer to the spirit and manner of early Donne than to any other poet. His admiration for Shakespeare is on record, but so qualified by changes of style and fashion that its consequence is difficult to locate in specific terms. The Shakespearean qualities in *The Goblins*, for example, are strangely transmuted. More of Suckling's poems show the direct influence of Donne or a reference to him than to anyone else, but Donne's intensities and complexities are always modulated, lightened, and detached in Suckling.

A similarity does not make an influence, and Robert Herrick and Sir John Suckling would seem poles apart. Where Herrick saw Mistress Susanna Southwell's feet as snails, Suckling saw Lady Anne Wentworth's feet as little mice. The difference is probably in Suckling's favor; in this instance he could match Herrick comfortably. Perhaps the similarity argues for no more than Suckling's catholicity of taste, but "A Ballade. Upon a Wedding," with its vigorous and innocent rural bawdry, and its gaiety, may point to Herrick in larger ways. Moreover, both Suckling and Herrick share an undeserved reputation for being more superficial than they really are. A certain darkness, an intense dissatisfaction with reality, a disappointed idealism, is beneath the surface of both poets.

Inevitably Suckling must be compared with his friend Thomas Carew and with his younger contemporary, Richard Lovelace. These three are the most substantial of the Cavalier poets, and it is this trio that comes to mind at the very word Cavalier. Suckling, of course, specifically criticizes Carew in "The Wits" for his "hard bound" muse and does not mention Lovelace, who did not move in the circle celebrated in the poem. Lovelace's muse was scarcely "hard bound" as Joseph H. Summers describes him, "he has little sense of structure and his syntax is sometimes shaky or hopelessly wrenched."[12] Suckling is a far better and more conscious craftsman than Lovelace. Beyond this, Lovelace is a poet who writes his best poems within the accepted conventions of the day. "To Lucasta, Going to the Warres," "To Amarantha, that she would deshevell her haire," "To Althea, From Prison," his best-remembered poems, achieve their particular strengths because of Lovelace's control of the conventions, because in them he accepts the pose and posture of the ideal of the Cavalier. In poems like "To a Lady that desired me I would beare my part with her in a Song" and "La Bella Bona Roba" Lovelace can strike a more robust note reminiscent of Suckling, but his usual inclination is to more highly conceited, Italianate poetry and to the use of the pastoral convention. Lovelace, moreover, is more solemn, more weighty than Suckling. "The Grasshopper" is the sort of traditional, classically influenced poem of wit and compliment that Suckling chooses not to write. In fact, most of Lovelace's poetry is exactly the kind Suckling is not only uninterested in but actively opposed to. For Suckling Lovelace's pastoral-Sidneian vein is old hat. Their agreement is to be found only when Lovelace drops the conventional poses of heroic and Arcadian love to write cynical and libertine verse.

Suckling celebrates his friendship with Carew in "Upon T. C. having the P., " "Upon my Lady Carliles walking in Hampton-Court garden," and in "The Wits." But the last two poems establish the critical differences between them. The argument in "Upon my Lady Carliles . . ." is that Carew writes within the accepted conventions of love poetry; in "The Wits," that Carew's poetry is too labored, "seldom brought forth but with trouble and pain" (73, 36), lacking in the freedom and ease Suckling admired. C. V. Wedgwood has written that "the truth was that the poets of his period, however young, and fashionable, belonged to the *arrière*, not to the *avant garde*. Their whole trend of thought reached back into a receding past, away from the cold and probing realism. . . ."[13] The observation is far more valid for Carew than for Suckling; in fact, it points to a major difference between them. A part of Suckling's objection to Carew's poetry is exactly that it is old-fashioned; it lacks the kind of modernity he himself espoused.

Carew's most popular poem, at least in the seventeenth century, "The Rapture," is a lively libertine performance in the witty Ovidian vein. It frequenty suggests Donne, and its cynicism and wit at least would appeal to Suckling. The poems admired today were probably not what Suckling had in mind when he criticized Carew. "An Elegie upon the death of the Deane of Pauls, Dr. John Donne" is a brilliant poem, a work of notable criticism, and a masterful imitation of Donne's style. Carew holds allegiance to both Donne and Jonson and "To Ben. Jonson. Upon occasion of his Ode of defiance annext to his play of the new Inne" effectively demonstrates his Jonsonian side and his perceptive, measured, and honest critical stance. "To my friend G. N. from Wrest" is a dignified and ceremonious poem in the tradition of Jonson's "To Penshurst." One would rather think that Suckling had in mind less-distinguished poems than these, poems more on the conventional order of "The Spring," "Celia *bleeding, to the Surgeon*," or "A Pastoral Dialogue." But even the former poems do mark Carew's substantial differences from Suckling. When Sir John wanted to express himself seriously, he turned to prose, not verse. Suckling rejects the conventional and traditional in Carew and is himself not interested in writing the kind of serious and substantial poetry Carew reached at his best. Inevitably what distinguishes Suckling from Lovelace and Carew is Suckling's amused distance from convention and his relaxed, informal style, his almost obstinate *sprezzatura*—in short, his "easiness."

III *Achievement*

A production of *Aglaura*, *The Goblins*, or *Brennoralt* today would be a delightful eccentricity possible only under the auspices of a university, but that another audience will ever thrill again to the cry of "I'm still *Brennoralt*" is unlikely in the extreme. Still, as has been noted, *Aglaura* and *Brennoralt* were theatrical successes in their own day, and all three plays were popular enough to be revived in the Restoration. The plays represent the breadth of Suckling's dramatic abilities. He could write with real competence in a variety of styles and was good enough to annoy a professional playwright like Richard Brome. It is impossible to predict where Suckling's skill with realistic comic dialogue might have taken him had he lived longer and had the chance to continue writing plays, but that skill is undeniable. The most accessible and easily appreciated aspects of Suckling's dramatic achievement are his abilities to write vivid, colloquial, realistic comic dialogue and to create effective short comic scenes, independent "turns." His stage language, moreover, forecast and gave a model to that of his successors in the Restoration. The pity is that he was not allowed to develop his full potentiality as a playwright.

As a prose stylist, too, Suckling looks forward to the coming age. The letters in particular show him the master of a witty, graceful, and colloquial prose style. His comic sense is delightfully illustrated in the letters. The amount of prose is limited, but its quality is high. Again, it is to be regretted that fate gave him so little time in which to exercise his talents.

But what finally can be said for Suckling as a poet? Poems such as the three "Sonnets," especially "Sonnet II" ("Of thee (kind boy) I ask no red and white"), "Loves Feast" ("I pray thee spare me, gentle Boy"), "The Constant Lover" ("Out upon it, I have lov'd"), "Song" ("Why so pale and wan fond Lover"), and "A Ballade. Upon a Wedding" are thoroughly alive and represent an undeniable poetic achievement. Suckling is admittedly never weighty; the philosophically serious and the emotionally intense are not his bent. The closest he gets to poetic seriousness is when his cynicism sometimes dominates his humor. Instead of the serious and intense or, for that matter, the purely lyric (there are other poets for those qualities), Suckling produced a poetry which, at its best, countered affectation with laughter and set a standard of civilized, controlled spontaneity. He could be as elegant as any of his fellow courtier poets, but he used his elegance ironically, playing against it his mastery of the colloquial. The colloquial voice served brilliantly to debunk a variety of poses, but it also offered itself as another sort of pose.

"Colloquial, " "controlled spontaneity," and similar descriptions are, of course, really just variations on "Natural, easy Suckling." The rightness of Congreve's description is inescapable. An ironic gaiety, a denial of elaborate artifice, an artful colloquialism, and a sense of comic detachment all contribute to that "naturalness" and "ease."

If he must be placed in some Parnassian hierarchy of seventeenth-century poets, his place is among the first poets of the second rank. He stands with Carew, Lovelace, and Davenant, but he is more than just another Cavalier poet. It is tempting to linger on the poignancy of early death, on the sensibility which both caught and mocked the "little know-not-whats, in faces," on the disappointed idealism which Ernest Rhys tagged in the phrase "Blood upon his gay feathers." But to linger too long is to miss his real achievement, the urbane comedy, the sense of perspective, the creation of a poetic voice which resulted in a style extending beyond the words themselves. He had the makings of a great comic artist; he died too soon.

Notes and References

Preface

1. I have also adopted Clayton's titles for untitled poems, but in the interest of simplicity have dropped the brackets which Clayton used to indicate that the title is not Suckling's.

Chapter One

1. London, 1675, p. 16.
2. James William Flosdorf, "The Poetry of Sir John Suckling: A Study of His Versification, Rhetoric, and Themes" (unpublished Ph.D. thesis, University of Rochester, Rochester, N. Y., 1960), p. ii.
3. *The Works of Sir John Suckling, The Non-Dramatic Works*, ed. Thomas Clayton (Oxford, 1971), p. 51, 11. 1 - 5. All quotations of Suckling are from this volume or from *The Works of Sir John Suckling, The Plays*, ed. L. A. Beaurline (Oxford, 1971), hereinafter referred to as Clayton and as Beaurline. As appropriate, page number, line and page number, or act, scene, and line number are indicated in parentheses in the body of the text.
4. *English Lyric Poetry* (London, 1913), p. 211.
5. " 'Why So Pale and Wan': An Essay in Critical Method," *University of Texas Studies in Literature and Language*, IV:4 (1963), 553.
6. *The Complete Poems of William Butler Yeats* (New York, 1951), p. 293.
7. Flosdorf, p. ii.
8. Clayton, p. 6.
9. "In answer of an Elegiacall Letter upon the death of the King of Sweden from Aurelian Townsend, inviting me to write on that subject," *The Poems of Thomas Carew*, ed. Rhodes Dunlap (Oxford, 1949), p. 77.
10. "A Life of Sir John Suckling" (unpublished doctoral dissertation, University of Nebraska, Lincoln, Nebraska, 1953), p. 61. My account of Suckling's life is based on Berry's dissertation, material in *Sir John Suckling's Poems and Letters From Manuscript*, ed. Herbert Berry (University of Western Ontario Studies in the Humanities, 1, 1960), and on Clayton's discussion of the life of Suckling in *Works*.
11. *An Account of the English Dramatic Poets* (Oxford, 1691), p. 138.

12. *Lives of the Poets of Great Britain and Ireland* (London, 1753), I, 294.

13. Berry, "Life," p. 45.

14. Berry, *Letters*, p. 49.

15. *Ibid.*, p. 50.

16. Clayton, p. xxxiii.

17. *Brief Lives*, ed. Oliver Lawson Dick (Ann Arbor, 1957), p. 287.

18. Aubrey, p. 287.

19. Berry, "Life," p. 100.

20. Aubrey, p. 288.

21. Berry, "Life," p. 153.

22. G. E. Bentley, *The Jacobean and Caroline Stage* (Oxford, 1956), V, 1202.

23. "Upon Aglaura in Folio," Clayton, p. 202.

24. Aubrey, pp. 289 - 90.

25. Berry, "Life," p. 196.

26. Berry, *Letters*, p. 104.

27. Clayton, p. xxxii.

28. Aubrey, p. 288.

29. "Sir *John* got on a bonny browne Beast," *Vox Borealis: Or the Northern Discoverie* (1641), Clayton, p. 207.

30. Berry, "Life," p. 256.

31. Beaurline, p. 176.

32. *The King's Peace* (London, 1955), p. 390.

33. *The Poems of Richard Lovelace*, ed. C. H. Wilkinson (Oxford, 1930), p. 82.

34. Clayton, p. lvii.

35. Aubrey, p. 290

Chapter Two

1. Letter No. 55, Clayton, p. cxiv, says the letter is "worth printing as possibly though not very probably by Suckling." It is stylistically very unlike Suckling.

2. *A Literary History of England*, ed. Albert C. Baugh (New York, 1948), p. 659.

3. For the detailed argument see Clayton, pp. 314 - 16. The reference to Van Dyck in the passage quoted from the letter might be construed as supporting a later date. Van Dyck painted Suckling probably between 1636 and 1639. However, the reference does not necessarily imply being painted by Van Dyck, and Suckling might have visited the artist's studio when he was in Europe.

4. Earl Morse Wilbur, *A History of Unitarianism in Transylvania, England, and America* (Cambridge, Massachusetts, 1952), p. 180. Clayton, p. 337, has a full and useful note on Socinianism.

5. Aubrey, p. 85.

6. H. John McLachlan, *Socinianism in Seventeenth-Century England*, p. 65, n. 2, quoted by Clayton, p. 337.

7. Morse, p. 183.

Chapter Three

1. Beaurline, p. vii.

2. *The Plays and Poems of William Cartwright*, ed. G. Blakemore Evans (Madison, 1951), p. 172.

3. Alfred Harbage, *Cavalier Drama* (New York, 1936), p. 14.

4. Walter Montague, *The Shepheard's Paradise* (London, 1659), p. 6.

5. *Ibid.*, p. 114.

6. The court influence on the drama and *préciosité* and court platonism are fully discussed in Alfred Harbage, *Cavalier Drama*, and Kathleen Lynch, *The Social Mode of Restoration Comedy* (New York, 1926).

7. Harbage, p. 36.

8. Beaurline, p. 3.

9. Harbage, p. 28.

10. Aubrey, p. 290.

11. Beaurline, pp. 253 - 63, and Clayton, pp. xliv - xlv provide the details of production, printing, the manuscript, etc.

12. Gerard Langbaine, *An Account of the English Dramatic Poets* (Oxford, 1691), p. 497.

13. *The Diary of Samuel Pepys*, quoted in Bentley, V, 1202, as is the following quotation.

14. Beaurline, p. 263.

15. Fredson Bowers, *Elizabethan Revenge Tragedy* (Princeton, 1966), p. 242.

16. Beaurline, p. 254.

17. *Ibid.*, pp. 255 - 56. The points made by Professor Beaurline in his commentary on *Aglaura* provide the basic suggestions for the position taken here.

18. Harbage, p. 111.

19. *Critical Essays of the Seventeenth Century*, ed. J. E. Spingarn (Oxford, 1908), II, 92.

20. Beaurline, pp. 255 - 56.

21. Aubrey, p. 290.

22. Beaurline, p. 261. The drawing is the frontispiece for Beaurline's edition.

23. *An Essay of Dramatic Poesy, Essays of John Dryden*, ed. W. P. Ker (Oxford, 1926), I, 81.

24. Lynch, p. 72.

25. *The Complete Poetry of John Donne*, ed. John T. Shawcross (New York, 1967), p. 134.

26. *The Platonic Lovers* (II, i), *The Dramatic Works of Sir William Davenant*, ed. James Maidment and W. H. Logan (Edinburgh and Lon-

don, 1872 - 74), II, 43.

27. " 'Why So Pale and Wan': An Essay in Critical Method," *University of Texas Studies in Literature and Language*, IV (1963), 553 - 63.

28. Beaurline, p. 270, cites W. R. Bowden, *The English Dramatic Lyric 1603 - 1642* (Yale Studies in English, vol. 118, 1951) for this concept.

Chapter Four

1. Beaurline, p. 274
2. *Diary*, May 22, 1667, quoted by Bentley, V, 1211.
3. *History of Dramatic Literature to the Death of Queen Anne* (London,1899) II, 349.
4. "Suckling's Imitation of Shakespeare," *Review of English Studies*, XIX (1943), p.290.
5. *Ibid.*
6. Quoted in Richard Ellman, *Yeats, The Man and the Masks* (New York, 1958), p. 278.
7. The history of the play's publication and production comes from Beaurline, pp. 288 - 94, and Bentley, V, 1207 - 1209.
8. Beaurline, p. 289, states that Herbert Berry, Suckling's biographer, believes so.
9. *Diary*, March 5, 1667 / 8, quoted by Bentley, V, 1208.
10. Harbage, p. 113.
11. Beaurline, p. 299.
12. R. J. Kaufman, *Richard Brome, Caroline Playwright*, "Suckling's New Strain of Wit" (New York and London, 1961), 151 - 68.

Chapter Five

1. The doubtful poems include ones long thought of as Suckling's, including "I prethee send me back my heart," "(Upon the Black Spots worn by my Lady D.E.)," and "Inconstancie in Woman," but a discussion of attribution is not deemed appropriate here. The reader is referred to Clayton, pp. lxxxvi - xciv, cv - cxiv, 290 - 301.
2. *The Cavalier Poets*, ed. Robin Skelton (New York, 1970), p. 28
3. Clayton, p. 3.
4. Reprinted in Clayton, p. 193.
5. Lord Dudley North, "Concerning Petty Poetry" in *Literary Criticism of Seventeenth-Century England*, ed. Edward W. Taylor (New York, 1967), p.159.
6. North, p. 160.
7. *Essays*, ed. W. P. Ker (Oxford, 1900), II, 191
8. North, p. 160.
9. *Ibid.* p. 159.
10. *Ibid.* p. 163.
11. "The Canon of Sir John Suckling's Poems," *Studies in Philology*,

LVII (1960), 492 - 518, and "New Poems by Sir John Suckling," *Studies in Philology*, LIX (1962), 653 - 55; Clayton, pp. xcix - ci.

12. Clayton, p. 230.
13. *Ibid.* p. 231.
14. L. A. Beaurline, "'Why So Pale and Wan': An Essay in Critical Method," *University of Texas Studies in Literature and Language*, IV (1963), 557.
15. Clayton, p. 232.
16. *Versions of the Baroque* (New Haven and London, 1972), p.93.
17. Warnke, p. 99.
18. Beaurline, p. 251.
19. *The Complete Poetry of Ben Jonson*, ed. William B. Hunter, Jr. (New York, 1963), p. 125.
20. *The Elegies and The Songs and Sonnets*, ed. Helen Gardner (Oxford, 1965), p. 21. The notes on p. 138 indicate the relation of "The Anagram" to Tasso's "Sopra la belleza" and the larger tradition of the "paradoxical encomium."

Chapter Six

1. Berry, "Life," pp. 104 - 53; Clayton, pp. xxxiii - xlii.
2. Clayton, p. 296.
3. Gardner, p. 34.
4. The libertine tradition is discussed by Fletcher Henderson, "Traditions of *Précieux* and *Libertin* in Suckling's Poetry," *ELH*, 4 (1937), 274 - 98. James Flosdorf argues in his unpublished dissertation "The Poetry of Sir John Suckling: *A Study of His Versification, Rhetoric, and Themes*" (University of Rochester, 1960) that Suckling is not a *libertin*. He finds the "Against Fruition" poems and the like to be within the courtly-love tradition, but any poem against a tradition can be viewed as being within the tradition. The deciding factor is the use to which the tradition is put. Suckling uses it disparagingly.
5. Gardner, p. 47.
6. *The Divine Comedy. Cantica I. Hell*, tr. Dorothy L. Sayers (Harmondsworth, Middlesex, 1949), Canto V. ll. 40 - 46, p. 98.
7. For a discussion of the authorship and relation to Matthew see Clayton, pp. xci - xcii and pp. 254 - 257.
8. "'Why So Pale and Wan': An Essay in Critical Method," *University of Texas Studies in Literature and Language*, IV (1963), 559 - 60.
9. T. S. Eliot, *The Complete Poems and Plays* (New York, 1952), p. 32.
10. "The Failure of Love: Love Lyrics after Donne," *Metaphysical Poetry, Stratford-Upon-Avon Studies*,11 (London, 1970), p. 58.

Chapter Seven

1. *The Life of Edward Earl of Clarendon* (Oxford, 1760), I, 41.

2.*Ibid.* The synod was held to discuss the question of the so-called Remonstrants, Dutch Protestants of the liberal wing of Calvinism.

3. Aubrey, p. 118.

4. A. R. Benham in "Sir John Suckling, A Sessions of the Poets' Some Notes and Queries," *Modern Language Quarterly,*VI (1945), discusses the relation of the poem to the poet laureateship and concludes "that in 1636 and 1637 there was at least some interest in the election of a poet laureate in England" (p. 25).

5. Alfred Harbage, *Sir William Davenant* (Philadelphia, 1935), p. 35.

6. Clarendon, I, 53.

7. George Garrard in a letter to the Earl of Stratford quoted in Clayton, p. xliv.

8. J. F. Bradley and J. Q. Adams, *The Jonson Allusion-Book* (New Haven, 1927),p. 187.

9. Clayton, p. 266.

10. *Ibid.*, p. 276.

11. Philip H. Gray, "Suckling's *A Sessions of the Poets* as a Ballad: Boccalini's 'Influence' Examined," *Studies in Philology*, XXXVI (1939), 60 - 69, concludes that Suckling was not influenced by Boccalini's *Ragguagli di Parnaso* and places "The Wits" in the ballad tradition.

12. The form is discussed in detail by Flosdorf, pp. 54 - 55.

13. *The Complete Poetry of Ben Jonson*, ed. William B. Hunter, Jr. (New York, 1963), p. 376.

14. "On the Time-Poets" in *Choyce Drollery*, ed. J. W. Ebsworth (Boston, Lincolnshire, 1876), p. 3.

15. Clayton, p. 267.

16. Ibid,. p. 268.

17. Berry, *Letters*, pp. 11 - 18, argues convincingly for the connection with Lord Lovelace and Lady Anne Wentworth rather than the earlier association with the. wedding of Roger Boyle, Lord Broghill. The "Dick" to whom the poem is addressed may be, as has often been suggested, Richard Lovelace, the poet and distant relative of the bridegroom, but there is no solid evidence.

18. *The Poems of Thomas Carew*, ed. Rhodes Dunlap (Oxford, 1949), p. 115.

19. *The Complete Poetry of Robert Herrick*, ed. J. Max Patrick (New York, 1968), p. 258.

20. Berry, *Letters*, p.15.

21. Herbert Berry (*Letters*, p. 15) argues for Jack Barry, "a fellow officer in the King's army. Barry had stood as Broghill's second in a duel less than a year before over another woman." Clayton (289) finds "the cynical Jack Bond . . . equally likely."

22. Berry, *Letters, p.* 15.

Chapter Eight

1. Clayton, p. 192. Clayton discusses Suckling's reputation on pp. lxiv - lxxv.

2. Robert Baron, *Pocalia Castalia*, 1650, in Clayton, p. lxviii.

3. Preface to *Letters and Poems, Amorous and Gallant*, quoted by George Williamson, *The Proper Wit of Poetry* (London, 1961), p. 108.

4. Theophilus Cibber, *Lives of the Poets of Great Britain and Ireland* (London, 1753), I, 295.

5. David Masson, *The Life of John Milton* (London, 1881), I, 503.

6. *The Poems of Sir John Suckling*, ed. Frederick A. Stokes (New York, 1886), p. xiv.

7. F. W. Moorman, "Cavalier Lyrists," *Cambridge History of English Literature* (Cambridge, 1911), VII, 23.

8. George Saintsbury, *A History of English Literature* (London, 1905), p. 376.

9. *A Literary History of England*, ed. Albert C. Baugh (New York, 1948), pp. 658 - 59.

10. *Everyone But Thee and Me* (Boston, Toronto, 1962), p.56

11. North, p. 166.

12. *The Heirs of Donne and Jonson* (London, 1970), p. 49.

13. *Velvet Studies* (London, 1946), p.23.

Selected Bibliography

PRIMARY SOURCES

Aglaura. London: Thomas Walkley, 1638.

The Discontented Colonell. London: Francis Eaglesfield, n. d.

Fragmenta Aurea. London: Humphrey Moseley, 1646.

The Last Remains of Sir John Suckling. London: Humphrey Moseley, 1659.

Sir John Suckling's Poems and Letters from Manuscript. Ed. Herbert Berry. London, Ontario: *University of Western Ontario Studies in the Humanities,* 1960.

Aglaura. London: Thomas Walkley, 1638; facsimile reprint, London: Scolar Press, 1970.

The Works of Sir John Suckling, The Non-Dramatic Works. Ed. Thomas Clayton. Oxford: Oxford University Press, 1971.

The Works of Sir John Suckling, The Plays. Ed. L. A. Beaurline. Oxford: Oxford University Press, 1971.

SECONDARY SOURCES

ANSELMENT, RAYMOND A. " 'Men Most of all Enjoy, When Least They Do': The Love Poetry of Sir John Suckling." *University of Texas Studies in Literature and Language,* XIV (1972), 17 - 32. A useful and perceptive study which puts Suckling's "cynicism" in perspective.

BEAURLINE, L. A. " 'Why So Pale and Wan': An Essay in Critical Method." *University of Texas Studies in Literature and Language,* IV (1963), 553 - 63. A stimulating approach to the critical problems raised by simple as opposed to complex poetry.

BENTLEY, GERALD EADES. *The Jacobean and Caroline Stage.* Oxford: Oxford University Press, 7 vols., 1940 - 1968. A monumental work, basic to the study of Jacobean and Caroline drama.

BERRY, HERBERT. "A Life of Sir John Suckling." Unpublished Ph.D. thesis. Lincoln, Nebraska: University of Nebraska, 1953. A most valuable study, to be supplemented by the life in *The Non-Dramatic Works.*

FLETCHER, J. B. *"Précieuses* at the Court of Charles I." *Journal of Comparative Literature,* I (1903), 120 - 53. An early background study of literary fashions at court.

FLOSDORF, JAMES WILLIAM. "The Poetry of Sir John Suckling: A Study of His Versification, Rhetoric, and Themes." Unpublished Ph.D. thesis.

Rochester, New York: University of Rochester, 1960. Especially informative regarding technical aspects of Suckling's poetry.

FREEHAFER, JOHN. "*The Italian Night Piece* and Suckling's *Aglaura*." *Journal of English and Germanic Philology*, LXVII (1968), 249 - 65. *Aglaura's* role in the history of changeable stage scenery.

HARBAGE, ALFRED. *Cavalier Drama*. New York: Modern Language Association of America, 1936. Highly useful historical and critical discussion of the drama and dramatic milieu of the period.

HENDERSON, F. O. "Traditions of *Précieux* and *Libertin* in Suckling's Poetry." *English Literary History*, IV (1937), 274 - 96. A helpful background commentary on literary fashions, asserting Suckling's libertine position.

LYNCH, KATHLEEN. *The Social Mode of Restoration Comedy*. New York: Macmillan, 1927. Especially valuable in its delineation of the social and intellectual background of the drama.

MARTZ, LOUIS L. *The Wit of Love*. Notre Dame, Indiana: University of Notre Dame Press, 1969. Four essays on Donne, Crashaw, Carew, and Marvell. The essay on Carew is useful for a reading of Suckling. Handsomely illustrated.

MINER, EARL. *The Cavalier Mode from Jonson to Cotton*. Princeton: Princeton University Press, 1971. A very helpful analysis of the major themes and attitudes defining the Cavalier mode. The chapters on "The Social Mode" and "Love" are especially pertinent to Suckling.

RICHMOND, HUGH M. *The School of Love: The Evolution of the Stuart Love Lyric*. Princeton: Princeton University Press, 1964. A scholarly analysis of the background and development of the love lyric.

SKELTON, ROBIN. *The Cavalier Poets*. "Writers and Their Work," No. 117. London: Longmans, Green, 1960. Critical appreciations of Suckling and his fellows.

SMITH, A. J. "The Failure of Love: Love Lyrics after Donne." *Metaphysical Poetry, Stratford-Upon-Avon Studies*, 11 (1970), 41 - 71. A perceptive discussion of changing attitudes toward love as seen in the lyrics after Donne.

SUMMERS, JOSEPH H. *The Heirs of Donne and Jonson*. London: Chatto and Windus, 1970. Examines the poetic heritage of Donne and Jonson and devotes part of a chapter to Suckling's relationship to them.

WALLERSTEIN, RUTH. "Suckling's Imitation of Shakespeare," *Review of English Studies*, XIX (1943), 290 - 95. *The Goblins* as exemplifying a Caroline view of Shakespeare's dramatic art.

WALTON, GEOFFREY. "The Cavalier Poets." *From Donne to Marvell*. Ed. Boris Ford. London: Penguin Books, 1956. Brief survey of the Cavaliers, with a negative glance at Suckling.

WARNKE, FRANK J. *Versions of Baroque, European Literature in the Seventeenth Century*. New Haven and London: Yale University Press, 1972. A scholarly analysis of the elements of the baroque style which provides a useful perspective for Suckling and the Cavalier poets.

WEDGWOOD, C. V. "Cavalier Poetry and Cavalier Politics." *Velvet Studies.* London: J. Cape, 1946. Valuable social and critical commentary on the Cavalier world.

Index

Aglaura, identity of, 27
Aubrey, John: *Brief Lives*, 22, 23, 25, 31, 63, 68, 138

Balzac, Jean Louis Guez de: *Lettres*, 34; *New Epistles of Monsieur de Balzack*, 48
Beaurline, L. A., 14, 67, 68, 73, 98, 103, 130
Berkeley, Sir William: *The Lost Lady*, 140
Berry, Herbert, 17, 145
Boisrobert, François le Metel de: *Le Couronnement de Darie*, 67
Bold, Henry, 118, 152
Bowers, Fredson, 66
Breton, Nicholas: *Post With a Mad Packet of Letters*, 34, 52
Brome, Richard, 25; *The Court Beggar*, 94
Brooke, Tucker, 33, 151
Buckingham, Duke of, 61, 62, 100

Callot, Jacques: *Miseries of War*, 133
Camus, Jean Pierre: *L'Iphigene*, 85
Carew, Thomas, 16, 28, 51, 108, 111, 138, 140, 153 - 54: "An Hymeneall Song on the Nuptials of the Lady Ann Wentworth and the Lord Lovelace," 143; "To my friend G. N. from Wrest," 136
Carleton, Sir Dudley, 137
Cartwright, William: *The Royal Slave*, 58, 68
Cary, Lucius, Lord Falkland, 43, 136, 139, 141
Cavalier, 13, 16, 62
Cavalier poets, 97, 151, 153
Chillingworth, William, 43, 138, 139; *The Religion of Protestants a Safeway of Salvation*, 46

Cibber, Theophilus, 18, 150
Clayton, Thomas, 17, 24, 110
Congrave, William: *The Way of the World*, 13, 14, 128, 150
Cranfield, Lionel. See Middlesex, Earl of

Dante: *Divine Comedy:* 127 - 128
Dario Coronato, 67
Davenant, Sir William, 25, 28, 43, 69, 138, 139, 156; *The Platonic Lovers*, 72, 79
Digby, Sir John, 23
Digby, Sir Kenelm, 23, 139
Donne, John, 71, 152 - 53; "The Anagram," 112; "Communitie," 124; "The Curse," 112; "Ecclogue 1613," 132; "The Extasie," 113; "Farewel to Love," 132; "Loves Deitie," 71, 125; "Womans Constancy," 102
Dort, Synod of, 137
drama, court, 57 - 60
Drayton, Michael: "The Sacrifice to Apollo," 141
Dryden, John, 69; *Discourse concerning the Original and Progress of Satire*, 99; *The Wild Gallant*, 65 - 66

Eliot, T. S.: "Whispers of Immortality," 132
Evans, G. Blakemore, 58

Flecknoe, Richard, 68
Fletcher, John 62; *The Sea Voyage*, 80
Flosdorf, James, 13, 16
Ford, John, 62

Godolphin, Sidney, 140
Goring, Colonel George, 31, 85
Gustavus Adolphus, 21

Hales, John, 43, 136, 137, 138, 139
Harbage, Arthur, 90
Henrietta Maria, 58, 139, 140
Herrick, Robert, 144, 153
Howell, James: *Epistolae Ho-Elianae*, 34
Hyde, Edward, Earl of Clarendon, 136, 139

Jonson, Ben, 61, 63, 138, 139, 140, 142, 152; "A Celebration of Charis," 106, 107
Johnson, Samuel, 142
Jones, Inigo, 68

Langbaine, Gerard, 18, 64
libertine, 117, 118, 122 - 23, 124, 127, 129
Lovelace, Richard, 28, 153 - 154
Lynch, Kathleen, 69

Masson, David, 150
Matthew, Sir Toby, 141
May, Thomas, 138, 139
Middlesex, Earl of, 17, 20, 21, 33, 35 - 36, 83
Montague, Walter: *The Shepherd's Paradise*, 58 - 60, 140
Moorman, F. W., 150
Moseley, Humphrey, 16
Murray, William, Earl of Dysart, 138

Nabbes, Thomas, 26; *Covent Garden*, 135
Nash, Ogden, 151
New Yorker, The, 152
North, Lord Dudley, 27; "Concerning Petty Poetry," 98 - 99

Pauline, James, 149
Pepys, Samuel: *Diary*, 64, 76, 90
Petrarchan tradition, 115, 127, 131
Phillips, Edward: *Theatrum Poetarum*, 13
Platonic love, 106, 127
Platonism, court, 59, 71, 72, 131
Plutarch: *Life of Artaxerxes*, 67

Quintilian: *Institutes of Oratory*, 103

Randolph, Thomas: "The milk-maids Epithalamium," 146
Rhys, Ernest, 14
Rochester, Earl of, 133
Rowe, Nicholas, 140

Saintsbury, George, 151
Saint Sorlin, Jean Desmarets de: *Aspasie*, 67
Saltonstall, Wye, 26; *Ovid de Ponto*, 135
Sandys, George, 138
Selden, John, 138, 139
Shakespeare, William, 65, 140, 153; *As You Like It*, 79; *The Rape of Lucrece*, 101; *Richard III*, 100; *The Tempest*, 79; *Twelfth Night*, 79
Sidney, Sir Philip: *Arcadia*, 126
Skelton, Robin, 97
Smith, A. J., 133
Socinianism, 43
Socinus, 43
Suckling, John (father), 17, 18
Suckling, Martha (mother), 17
Suckling, Martha (sister), 17, 29, 47, 48
Suckling, Sir John, achievement, 155 - 56; appointed Gentleman of the Privy Chamber, 26; Army Plot, 17, 30 - 31; attempt at marriage, 23; brawling, 23; carrying dispatches, 21; compared to: Carew, 153 - 55, Lovelace, 153 - 54; death of father, 18; dramatic achievement, 94 - 95; early years, 17 - 18; elected to Parliament, 29; First Bishops' War, 28 - 29; gambling, 22, 24; influenced by: Donne, 152 - 53, Herrick, 153, Jonson, 152, Shakespeare, 79 - 81, 153; knighted, 20; Second Bishops' War, 29 - 30; suicide, 31; travel abroad, 19 - 21.

WORKS:
Fragmenta Aurea, 16, 55, 56, 97, 108, 110, 111, 138, 149, 151
Last Remains of Sir John Suckling, The, 16, 55, 56, 57, 60, 111

PLAYS:
Aglaura, 24, 57, 63 - 75, 135; language,

69 - 72; plot, 65 - 67; spectacle, 72 - 75; use of painted scenes, 69
Brennoralt, 30, 57; language, 92 - 94; plot, 85 - 89; political allusions, 90 - 82
Discontented Colonel, The. See *Brennoralt*
Goblins, The, 30, 57, influence of Shakespeare, 79 - 81; language, 83 - 84; plot, 76 - 79; satire, 82 - 83; scenes, 81 - 85; songs, 82, 84
Sad One, The, 24, 57, 60 - 63, 106

POEMS:
"Against Absence," 118 - 19
"Against Fruition I" (Stay here fond youth and ask no more, be wise"), 116 - 17
"Against Fruition II" ("Fye upon hearts that burn with mutual fire"), 117 - 18
"Answer, The," 128 - 29
"Ballade. Upon a Wedding, A," 135, 143 - 146, 148
"Barber, A," 101
"Candle, A," 101
"Careless, Lover, The," 126, 129 - 30
"Constant Lover, The" ("Out upon it, I have lov'd"), 128 - 29
"Deformed Mistress, The," 111 - 12
"Detraction execrated," 111, 112 - 13
"Disdain," 116
"Dreame, A," 100, 101
"Expostulation, The," 116
"Farewel to Love," 132 - 33
"His Dream," 101
"Invocation, The," 115
"Loves Feast" ("I pray thee spare me, gentle Boy"), 126 - 28
"Loves Offence," 97
"Loving and Beloved," 97
"Lutea Alison," 103 - 104
"On New-years day 1640. To the King," 30, 97
"Pedler of Small-wares, A," 101
"Perjury disdain'd," 102
"Prologue of the Author's to a Masque at Wiston, A," 57, 113
"Sessions of the Poets, A." See "The Wits"

"Soldier, A," 101
"Song" ("No, no faire Heretique"), 116
"Song to a Lute, A," 24, 106 - 108
"Song ("Why so pale and wan fond Lover?"), 24, 130 - 32
"Sonnet I" ("Do'st see how unregarded now"), 122 - 24
"Sonnet II" ("Of thee (kind boy) I ask no red and white"), 122, 124 - 25
"Sonnet III" ("Oh! for some honest Lovers ghost"), 122, 125 - 26
"Summons to Town, A," 136 - 38
"Supplement of an imperfect Copy of Verse of Mr. Will. Shakespears, By the Author, A," 101
"To a Lady that forbidd to love before Company," 121 - 22
"To his Rival I" ("My dearest Rival least our love"), 119 - 20
"To his Rival II" ("Now we have taught our Love to know"), 116, 119, 121
"To Mr. Davenant for Absence," 118, 119
"To Mr. W. M. Against Absence," 118, 119
"Upon A. M.," 105 - 106
"Upon Christmas," 100
"Upon My Lady Carliles walking in Hampton-Court garden," 24, 37, 108 - 11
"Upon my Lord Brohalls Wedding," 135, 146 - 48
"Upon St. Johns-day comeing after Christmas day," 100
"Upon T. C. having the P.," 111
"Upon the first sight of my Lady Seimor," 24
"The Wits," 25, 96, 98, 135, 138 - 43
"Womans Constancy" ("There never yet was woman made"), 126

PROSE:
Account of Religion by Reason, An," 25, 42 - 46, 100, 135
"Answer to a Gentleman in Norfolk that sent to enquire after the Scotish business," 28, 38 - 39
"Disswasion from Love, A," 51, 52 - 53
family letters, 46 · 49
"Letter to a friend to diswade him from

marrying a Widow, A," 51 - 52
letters to: Bulkeley, Mary, 54, 55;
Carew, Thomas, 51; Cranfield,
Mary, 54 - 55; "Ladies," 50 - 51;
"London Alderman," 141 - 142;
Middlesex, Earl of, 35 - 36; "Scottish
Lord," 140 - 141; Wallis, William,
49 - 50
"To a Cosin," 51, 53 - 54
"To Mr. Henry German, In the Begin-
ning of Parliament, 1640," 30, 39 -
41
"Wine-drinkers to the Water-drinkers,
greeting, The," 51
Summers, Joseph H., 153

Thompson, A. H., 150

D'Urfé, Honoré: *L'Astrée*, 59

Vane, Sir Henry, 21, 36
Vaughan, Sir John, 139

Waller, Edmund, 118, 138, 139, 152
Wallerstain, Ruth, 76
Walsh, William, 150
Ward, Sir A. W., 76
Warnke, F. J., 104
Wedgwood, C. V., 30
Wenman, Sir Francis, 139
Wilbur, Earl Morse, 46

Yeats, William Butler, 15, 81